Your Education Leadership Handbook

Jim McGrath & Anthony Coles

PEARSON

Harlow, England • London • New York • Boston • San Francisco • Toronto • Sydney • Auckland • Singapore • Hong Kong
Tokyo • Seoul • Taipei • New Delhi • Cape Town • São Paulo • Mexico City • Madrid • Amsterdam • Munich • Paris • Milan

Pearson Education Limited
Edinburgh Gate
Harlow
Essex CM20 2JE
England

and Associated Companies throughout the world

Visit us on the World Wide Web at:
www.pearson.com/uk

First published 2012

© Pearson Education Limited 2012

ISBN: 978-1-4082-8479-7

British Library Cataloguing-in-Publication Data
A catalogue record for this book is available from the British Library

Library of Congress Cataloging-in-Publication Data
McGrath, Jim.
  Your education leadership handbook / Jim McGrath and Anthony Coles.
     p. cm.
  Includes bibliographical references and index.
  ISBN: 978-1-4082-8479-7 (pbk.)
  1. Educational leadership--Handbooks, manuals, etc. 2. School management and organization--Handbooks, manuals, etc. 3. School administrators--Handbooks, manuals, etc.
I. Coles, Anthony. II. Title.
  LB2805.M334 2011
  371.2--dc23
                    2011036407

10 9 8 7 6 5 4 3 2 1
15 14 13 12 11

Typeset in 10/14 Arial Light by 30
Printed and bound in Malaysia, CTP-KHL

Contents

About the authors

Jim McGrath currently teaches education management and leadership and research skills on a number of undergraduate and postgraduate courses. As someone who obtained all his qualifications by part-time study, he has a particular commitment to non-traditional students.

Anthony Coles is Reader in Post-compulsory Education and Director of CPD for the Faculty of Education Law and Social Sciences at Birmingham City University. Much of his teaching involves research skills and supporting teachers in their professional development.

Also by the same authors:

Your Education Research Project Handbook

Your Teacher Training Handbook

Introduction

Why do you need this book?

It does seem that barely a week goes by without another book on education leadership appearing. So why is another one required, you may ask. Basically we had four reasons for writing this book. First, many leadership texts fail to take into account the external (policy) and internal (organisational culture) environment that education leaders operate in. In Tutorials 1 and 2 we explicitly explain how managerialism and organisational culture create the environment in which education leadership is exercised. Secondly, very often leadership books and training courses promote one particular approach to leadership and fail to critically evaluate the theory or theories they espouse. The first person narrative approach that we use provides rich opportunities for each theory to be critically evaluated as it is discussed by Dr Martin Vinick, a university lecturer, and Nat Lang, an experienced teacher. Thirdly, few general texts on leadership give any guidance on how the reader can use their knowledge to analyse and understand events in the workplace. By encouraging you to reflect upon the theories, past events and your own feelings, we aim to show how knowledge of theory can inform your understanding of management and leadership. Fourthly, many books misleadingly suggest that the reader only has to follow their formulaic guideline to become a leader. If only wishing made it so! Leadership is a much more complex process than that. If you attempt to apply one theory or set of guidelines in all circumstances, you will fail. Good leaders are true unto themselves. They have identified their beliefs and values and developed a personal management philosophy that informs their actions. We will encourage you, through a process of reflection, to identify the sort of leader you aspire to be. Armed with this self-knowledge you will be in a position to develop your own leadership style and to select the most appropriate tools from a range of theories and processes to meet the demands of leadership.

In essence, our intention was to produce a short, readable book which will provide you with the skills and knowledge necessary to:

- Understand how the internal and external environment in which education leaders operate curtails their freedom of action.
- Discuss and critically evaluate a wide range of leadership theories.
- Understand how to apply leadership theory.

- Identify and develop your own leadership style.
- Start to think about the ethical implications of leadership.

Our target audience is managers, leaders, teachers, trainers, lecturers, and mentors in all sectors of education who want to be a better leader. It will be especially useful for anyone studying management or leadership on an undergraduate, postgraduate or CPD course. With many years experience of teaching management and leadership to education students between us, we are convinced that the leadership issues faced by managers, staff and teachers are essentially the same regardless of which education sector they work in. Every educationalist operates within a target-driven culture. This is unlikely to change any time soon. Education has become too important politically for any government to abandon the monitoring of learners' performance. It is likely that in the years ahead even more will be demanded of teachers as the government seeks to improve quality and reduce costs.

The students we encounter are nearly always unaware of the managerialist revolution that started in the 1980s and which continues to largely determine the actions of managers and leaders in education and the wider public sector. Students assume that the management approaches adopted in the public sector are the same as those in the private sector and fail to realise that they operate in a quasi-market environment which is very different from the private sector and suffers from intrinsic contradictions. When this is understood, it becomes easier to understand the actions of education leaders. This knowledge will improve your professional practice and enable you to make the links between dry theory, governmental policy and actual practice.

Format and style of the book

The book is effectively a case study of one manager's experience over a three-month period. It takes the form of ten tutorials between an academic tutor Dr Martin Vinick and Nat Lang. The relationship is one of near colleagues and not the tutor/student relationship that existed in our previous books. Do not be discouraged if Nat appears to know more about management and leadership than you do. This is because Nat is an experienced teacher who already holds the management qualifications necessary to become a head teacher/principal. In preparation for this change in status, Nat wishes to critically evaluate a range of leadership theories as part of a continuous professional development programme (CPD). Nat intends to use this analysis to define more clearly a personal leadership style.

Prior to becoming a teacher, Nat worked in the private sector and local government as a finance officer. Since qualifying as a teacher Nat has worked in a number of schools and colleges and is currently a member of the Senior Management Team (SMT). Precisely which education sector Nat works in is never divulged. For that reason we always use the word principal rather than head teacher as this is a term that is becoming increasingly popular in schools (American teen movies with principals and proms have a lot to answer for). Nor do we reveal Nat's gender. We urge you to create your own back story for Nat.

In order to avoid the need to alternate between male and female pronouns when discussing the actions of principals, we have consistently used the female form. This, we feel, balances Martin's prominence in the text.

Building on the approach that we used in *Your Education Project Handbook* and *Your Teacher Training Handbook*, each chapter will consist of a verbatim record of the tutorial, interspersed with a series of reflections by Nat followed by space for you to make your own brief notes. Each tutorial will deal with an aspect of management or leadership, and the application of theory will be explored using reflection and discussion of past experiences. This approach is, we think, both entertaining and an excellent way to demonstrate how theory can be used in practice to explore and understand actual events. Additional material at the end of each tutorial will include:

- Nat's summary of the session.
- An evaluation of how what has been learnt will impact on Nat's leadership style.
- A diagrammatic representation of some of the key issues discussed.
- Selected handouts.
- Suggestions for further reading.

In addition to the above, a list of contents is provided at the start of each tutorial together with a short statement outlining the aims of the tutorial. However, the order of the contents is indicative only. This is because the nature of a tutorial means that the discussion may return to the same topic more than once and Nat's reflections are invariably retrospective.

A glossary of key terms is provided at the end of the book which you may wish to refer to for clarification. Each key term has been highlighted in the text when first used.

As the size of the book is limited, additional materials can be found at www.pearsoned.co.uk/mcgrathandcoles. These will include:

- Additional information on the theories discussed.
- A copy assignment at Master's level.
- Advice on how you might analyse the organisational culture of your school or college.
- Advice on how you might analyse the leadership style used in your school or college.
- Examples of leaders in action.
- Links to other useful websites.

The site is entirely free and we would urge you to have a look at it.

Tutorials 1 and 2 deal with the environment within which education leaders operate. Tutorial 1 discusses the limitations that are imposed on leaders in the education sector by government targets and policy and asks the question: to what extent can genuine leadership be exercised when external pressures constrain the leader's actions? Tutorial 2 explores the concept of organisational culture. A range of popular theories are considered, and the tutorial examines how organisation culture can influence and be influenced by a leader's actions.

Tutorial 3 discusses how leadership has replaced management as the panacea for solving the problems of the education sector and seeks to identify what, if any, the differences are between these contested terms. It then examines the claim that education leadership is different from leadership in other sectors, before ending with a discussion of the sources of power available to principals.

Tutorial 4 evaluates two theories that focus on the characteristics possessed by the leader. Trait theory is one of the oldest leadership theories in existence and is compared with the relatively new theory of emotional intelligence.

Tutorial 5 explores three popular leadership theories (style, contingency and situational). All three theories focus on what the leader does rather than on what characteristics or qualities (innate or learnt) they possess.

Tutorial 6 focuses on two theories that emphasise the idea that leadership is based upon a series of mutually beneficial exchanges between the leader and follower. These theories are leader member exchange (LMX) and transactional (TX).

Tutorial 7 evaluates charismatic (CL) and transformational (TL) leadership, both of which encourage followers to personally identify with the aims and objectives of the leaders, and explores why they have gained such prominence in the education sector since the 1990s.

Tutorial 8 explores the views of popular management gurus and evaluates distributed leadership (DL) which many commentators have suggested is the ideal vehicle for motivating staff and bringing about change in educational settings. Distributed leadership requires staff to share the burden of leadership and, to some extent, decision making.

Tutorial 9 explores what many believe is the key function of any leader, namely to lead change, and provides a model for thinking about the stages that staff go through when faced by significant change.

Tutorial 10 considers what ethical leadership is and contrasts this with Machiavelli's advice to *The Magnificent Lorenzo de Medici* on how a prince should rule. The tutorial ends with a brief outline of a range of behaviours that ethical leaders demonstrate.

How to use this book

If you are following a course on management or leadership, this book is not a replacement for any taught sessions that you might be attending. As Woody Allen said, 95 per cent of success is about turning up, so turn up to those all-important lectures and tutorials.

So how might you use the book?

- Read the relevant tutorial or tutorials before attending a taught session on the same issues. This will familiarise you with the key concepts and enable you to clarify anything that you are unsure of with your lecturer.

- Read the appropriate tutorial/s after a session. This will reinforce the learning that has already taken place and provide a different perspective on the issues.

- Use the summary of each tutorial's main points and/or the diagrams in each tutorial to identify and understand the key issues. Visual learners may wish to study the diagram before reading the relevant tutorial in order to obtain an overview of the key issues discussed.

- Use the analysis of the strengths and weaknesses of each leadership theory as the basis of your critical evaluation of specific theories.

- Use Nat's discussion on how the theories can be used as a starting point for the development of your own style, or to inform an existing leadership style.

- Use the book as a learning resource when you have missed a session or found discussion of a particular theory particularly challenging.

- Follow up the further reading recommendations provided at the end of each chapter.

We are conscious that long reading lists can demotivate rather than inspire readers and, for that reason, we have restricted our recommendations for further reading to a maximum of four texts at the end of each tutorial. When following up a reference, you should decide how much of the recommended text you need to read: some, most or all.

While the format of a tutorial has many advantages, it also provides us with two specific challenges. In order to maintain the narrative flow of a tutorial we have:

1. Refrained from giving a full reference for every idea discussed as this would result in a very stilted text. So, instead of Martin saying 'As Coles and McGrath (2010 page 3) argue …' we have written 'As Coles and McGrath argue …'. A full bibliography detailing all the texts referred to appears at the end of the book. **However, we wish to emphasise how important it is for students to fully reference any material that they use in their own assignments or dissertations**.

2. Rejected the suggestion from some reviewers that we supply subheadings within the tutorial in order to make it easier to find specific theories or ideas. Before making this decision we conducted a small-scale survey with students who had purchased our previous book on research. By a margin of 2:1 they felt that the use of subheadings would detract from the flow of the discussion. In order to find a specific topic you should use the index at the end of the book. For anyone studying at undergraduate or postgraduate level, learning to use the index effectively is a vital academic skill. Using the index is a far more effective way of finding material on a specific topic than any table of contents. The index can also save you the time and effort of reading through an entire chapter for maybe just a couple of paragraphs of essential information.

If you are studying for a management module, particularly at postgraduate level, it is essential that you get into the habit of reading journal articles. Not only are they the most up-to-date source for ideas but they are also peer reviewed, which means that their academic provenance can be vouched for.

We wish you the very best of luck in your chosen career, and if you have any suggestions for how we could make this book more useful to other students and managers, please contact us.

Anthony Coles
Jim McGrath
Birmingham City University, 2011

For Jane, Bea and William

For Eija, Helen and Michael with love. Also for all the McGrath's, Mom (Bridget), Dad (Ted), Alice, Tony, Fred, Alf, and little Vera and Michael.

Acknowledgements

I had the great pleasure and good fortune to study for my Doctor of Education at the University of Birmingham under three gifted teachers: Helen Gunter, Peter Ribbons and Des Rutherford. As my supervisor, Des taught me more than he will ever know; it is accurate to say that without his inspiration this book would never have been written. Thanks, Des, for everything.

Jim McGrath

We would also like to thank the many MA students who have unwittingly contributed to this book with their comments over the years and in particular, Leanne Flood, for her permission to publish her MA dissertation on Transformational Leadership on the website that accompanies this book. Also, thank you to our editors, Catherine Yates and Lauren Hayward, at Pearson Education for their continued support and encouragement; it is much appreciated.

Anthony Coles

Jim McGrath

Managerialism and control

Aim of tutorial

To help you understand the macro-environmental pressures that affect all managers and staff in the education sector.

Contents

- Bureau-professionalism
- The advent of managerialism
- Value for money (VFM)
- Managerialism
- Performativity

Note: As stated in the Introduction, the term 'principal' has been used throughout this book instead of head teacher or head mistress.

Nat's reflection

22 September

I'm not sure if I've done the right thing. Instead of spending my annual training allowance on a couple of conferences where I could enjoy a few days away from the problems of work I've 'bought' ten one-hour tutorials with Dr Martin Vinick at the local university. As I explained to him when we met, I have a lot of experience of management and leadership in both the private and public sectors. I've also undertaken numerous management development courses and even sat a few management examinations. But I've never had the time to critically evaluate the various theories and identify my own leadership style. Instead my leadership style has just grown and developed over the years without a lot of conscious thought. Now that I'm actively looking to become a principal, it's time I consciously examined my leadership style.

Martin suggested that as I didn't want or need a full course we should just meet for a series of one-to-one tutorials on the broad subject of education leadership. To get the most from the sessions Martin suggested that I should do a bit of reading before each session. For today's meeting he asked me to Google 'managerialism' and see what I could find. He said that if at a later stage I decide to pursue my studies the tutorials and the reading would give me enough information to write a good assignment at postgraduate level. We'll see.

He also suggested that I record each tutorial. That way I can reflect on what I have learnt and link any new learning to my previous experiences of leadership. Sounds reasonable to me.

Review of tutorial

When I arrived, Dr Vinick was thumbing through the latest edition of the British Educational Leadership, Management and Administration Society's (BELMAS) journal, his near-black hair, surprising in a man who was at least 60, bobbing up and down as he skim-read the pages. Looking up he smiled and said, '**Nice to see you. Would you like a cup of tea?**' His accent was unmistakably that of Yorkshire.

'That would be great,' I said and set up my recorder and unpacked my note pad as he made two teas and found a packet of biscuits that looked slightly the worse for wear.

'**OK,**' he said, '**As I understand it you have studied management and leadership over the years first as part of your accounting exams and recently a national training course for principals.**'

'I've also done numerous management development and training courses over the years,' I said.

'**Grand. So we can discuss these issues rather than me sit here and act as the all-wise guru dispensing words of wisdom. But I warn you, I won't be doing all the talking and I expect you to disagree with me on various issues. Don't hold back. I like a good argument. Deal?**'

'Deal,' I said.

'**Good. I'd like to start by looking at the external environment within which education leadership is exercised. I asked you to Google 'Managerialism'. What did you find out?**'

For a moment I was taken aback by the question. I had thought he'd ease me into the session but he was clearly taking no prisoners. Collecting my thoughts I replied, 'It was something that started in the 1980s and the idea was that public sector organisations, including schools, hospitals and the police, should be run and managed using techniques and practices that were common in the private sector.'

'**OK, that's not bad. Let's leave that for a minute. What do you think was the management culture in education prior to managerialism?**'

'Don't look at me', I said. 'I only started secondary school in 1976.'

'**Don't say that. It makes me feel so old,**' Martin said smiling.

'Well, speaking to "old timers at work",' I said teasingly, 'I'm told it was less hierarchical and more collegiate.'

'It's interesting how people embellish the past making it into some sort of golden age. The truth is that there was never a golden age of collegiality in schools, colleges or universities. People may have aspired to it but the idea that academics or teachers came together, discussed issues, and arrived at a decision that everyone agreed with is a fiction. There were always people jockeying for advancement in the organisation just as there were some teachers, administrators and leaders that exercised greater influence and control than others. But, very often, they did so covertly rather than overtly. If you want an example of what I mean read C.P. Snow's *The Masters*.'

'If collegiality didn't exist, what did?'

'It was called bureau-professionalism and it did contain an element of collegiality. Basically the attitudes, beliefs and values held by teachers and lecturers at the time were typified by an overriding concern for the students' learning and well-being and a belief that lecturers and teachers should be seen as a source of expertise. As a professional educator, your loyalty was not to the organisation you worked for but to your subject, the colleagues you worked with, the maintenance of academic standards and your students. This logically led to the belief that because managers, such as departmental heads or principals, were socialised within a particular profession or discipline, they should share the same values as their more junior colleagues. Therefore the relationship between the leader and led should be one based upon mutual trust, a respect for professional autonomy and a belief that accountability should be to peers not managers.'

'I don't see a lot of that in my organisation. There tends to be a "them and us" split between managers and staff.'

'We'll come to that in a moment. The final elements of this bureau-professional settlement was a commitment to public service, with the needs and rights of students being paramount and a belief that the quality of provision should be assessed on the basis of inputs not outputs.'

'Can you give me an example of these shared values in action?' I asked.

'Well, I worked at a school in the 80s where the teachers went on strike. I can't remember what the strike was about but I do remember the principal and his deputy taking out cups of tea to the pickets. Effectively they were saying "Because of our position we can't join you. But we support your fight". That wouldn't happen today.'

'So there was a feeling that everyone shared the same values and were all working towards a single goal. What happened to change it?'

'As with the idea of collegiality, bureau-professionalism was to some extent a fiction. A model that educationalists liked to think existed and certainly aspects of it did. But it was a model that many people disliked, including Margaret Thatcher, who became Prime Minister in 1979. Her ideology had its origins in the philosophies of "New Right" thinkers such as Milton Friedman. She was supported in her beliefs by her mentor Sir Keith Joseph and organisations like The Adam Smith Institute and the Centre for Policy Studies. Her argument was that from 1945 to 1979 education policy had been producer-led, with the teachers' unions, local education authorities and representatives of the Department for Education and Science forming what Ball called a "triangle of tension" that had excluded the concerns of consumers.'

'I can see how she might have thought that the model was overly paternal. A sort of "We're the experts, we know what's best for you".'

'Exactly. Mrs Thatcher sought to change the situation by giving more power to the consumers and excluding the producer lobby from the policy-making process. She had been Education Secretary in the 1970s and Ball believes that she was fighting for traditional educational values against the various isms that had crept into education such as progressivism, comprehensivism, egalitarianism, multiculturalism, pluralism and relativism.'

'So she decided to give greater prominence to the wishes of the consumer of education and hold the professionals to account?'

'Yes. This approach was inspired by the theories of James Buchanan and the school of Public Choice Theory (PCT) which he helped found. PCT argued that the market should be used as an instrument of regulation and control within the public sector. There is a good article on this by Olssen and Peters explaining how PCT was developed and applied. It's well worth reading.'

'So it was this policy that has led to teaching staff becoming subject to the system of controls, inspections and accountability that we live with today?'

'Basically, yes. Avis suggests that you can see just how all-pervasive the new approach has been by the extent to which the Labour Government in 1997 took on board the new educational settlement that developed between 1980 and 1997. He thinks that New Labour largely accepted the Conservatives' interpretation of such issues as the relationship between education, competitiveness and globalisation and the use of managerialist techniques including external inspection, targeted funding and league tables to control the public services.'

Nat's reflection

23 September

It's interesting how we just accept the situation we find ourselves in and don't question it. I've never really thought about the paradigm within which I operate as a teacher. I suppose I have just assumed that it has always been the way it is and it always will be. This is stupid really because along with death and taxes the one thing we can be certain of is change. The way schools are managed and led will change as different political parties come to power and emphasise different aspects of policy. Also, as society evolves, what are acceptable management practices will also change. After all, it's not so long ago that it was quite acceptable to pay a woman less than a man for doing the same job.

I do try to be alert to the changes that are going on in education at both a local and national level because what is a new approach today will be next year's must-implement initiative. But I should spend more time looking at what policy makers are talking about and try to work out how it will impact on my professional practice before it becomes something I have to implement immediately. Basically, I need to start thinking and acting strategically.

Space for your notes

Prompts

● Are there any vestiges left in your school of bureau-professional practices? If so, what are they?

● To what extent do you think your school is run like a business?

Review of tutorial

'So what are the defining characteristics of managerialism?' I asked.

'Well, for a start it's been called many different things since the 1980s, including: new public management, new managerialism, entrepreneurial governance and neo-Taylorism. We'll just call it managerialism. Power argues that what you have to understand is that managerialism is an ideology that is underpinned by two key notions, Universalism and Isomorphism. Universalism holds that all organisations are basically the same and should pursue efficiency as the best means of satisfying its customers. Isomorphism assumes that the structures associated with commercial organisations are the most natural and effective way to coordinate the production of goods and services.'

'If you accept that, then by definition all public sector organisations must be inefficient and they should be reorganised to look and act like private sector organisations,' I said.

'Exactly.'

'But that ignores the fact that there is a fundamental difference between public and private sector organisations.'

'**Go on,**' said Martin leaning forward.

'Private sector organisations have numerous targets and objectives. But their ultimate objective is to remain profitable and continue in business. Public sector organisations are not driven by the profit motive.' I paused, then carried on, 'Before I got into teaching I worked in a local government education department. Decisions were seldom made on the basis of profit and loss; they were made on the basis of how many votes they would win or lose. So it was not unusual for money to be spent repairing or renovating schools in key marginal wards prior to local elections. Every party did it. The councillors weren't motivated by profit or loss; their currency was votes at the next election. The public sector operates in a political environment, not a commercial for-profit environment.'

'I agree, and that is why the application of some managerialist approaches can cause problems. Now, if you worked in local government, you will know that the Audit Commission was established in 1983 under the provisions of the 1982 Local Government Finance Act. The Commission was one component in the Conservative strategy to control public expenditure and promote proper stewardship of public funds. In addition to traditional financial audits, the Commission was empowered to undertake Value for Money (VFM) audits in the public sector. Now, VFM consists of three interrelated concepts: economy, efficiency and effectiveness. Economy is concerned with obtaining goods and services of the required standard at least cost. Efficiency is concerned with maximising production of goods or services at the required standard from the least input, and effectiveness is a measure of how successful an organisation has been in achieving its objectives. The auditors were charged with examining all three concepts and reporting on how successful the authority had been in achieving them. Which of the three concepts do you think is most important?'

'Of the three I'd have to say effectiveness because it's pointless being economic and efficient if the organisation pursues the wrong objectives or fails to achieve its objectives.'

'I agree. Now VFM was but one component in the package of assumptions, techniques, ideas and behaviours that came to typify managerialism. Most importantly, the practice of management was raised above the importance of the function being managed and emphasis was placed on the manager's right to manage. Now, that is a very different view of the manager's role from the one that existed under bureau-professionalism. To emphasise this break with the past, there was a conscious effort to weaken trade union and professional ties within the workplace as a prelude to the creation of a more flexible workforce. In addition, appraisal systems and performance-related pay were introduced as a means of aligning the individual's aims and objectives more closely with those of the organisation.'

'I remember a colleague of mine who worked in a college during the 90s: he told me that, when colleges became free of local authority control, the new Further Education Funding Council threatened to reduce the grant paid to colleges unless colleges transferred staff over to new contracts of employment. Any staff that remained on the old "Silver Book" conditions of employment were to receive no annual increments to their salaries.'

'I've heard that myself. Of course, forcing managers to take such actions brought about the "them and us" split that you referred to earlier. Simkins believes that policy makers wanted to encourage just such a split. They wanted to separate managers from staff; that way it was easier to break down large-scale organisations into subunits which were then encouraged to view their relationships with other units in the organisation as a series of low-trust relationships linked not by professional values but by **quasi-contracts**.'

'So we are back to Buchanan's idea of managing schools and colleges like commercial organisations,' I said.

'Indeed we are.'

'I know what quasi means and what a contract is, but can you give me an example of what you mean by a quasi-contract?'

'For example, prior to the decentralisation of **budgets**, schools and the child psychology service had all been part of the same local authority. After decentralisation the school had to "purchase" psychology services from the local authority. The creation of these subunits, or **cost centres** as they are known, meant that it was possible to evaluate the efficiency of each unit by devolving to it a budget and then monitoring how much they spent against the budget allocated. Where an income budget was also devolved, they were known as **trading centres** because it became possible to calculate how much they had made or lost during the year by comparing income with expenditure. And of course along with budgets an extensive range of other **performance indicators** were introduced, all of which were intended to control staff activities and emphasise the manager's right to keep tabs on what the staff were doing and how they were performing.'

'Which is a long way from respecting colleagues as autonomous professionals,' I said. 'But, prior to the 1980s, attempts must have been made to control public sector spending in general and education in particular: why did managerialism succeed here where so many other attempts failed?'

'That's a really good question. It may have been a moment in history. The whole world seemed to change in the 80s and 90s. Capitalism defeated Soviet communism and the public bought into the idea that the private sector model of management and control was superior to that which existed in the public sector. But if I had to pick one reason I'd say that unlike previous reforms, which had been directed at the macro level, Mrs Thatcher recognised the value of targeting reform at the micro or institutional level. This required the use of detailed regulations that defined the "rules of the game", the incentives available for success, the penalties for failure and the performance criteria by which institutions would be judged. This policy was then operationalised by such organisations as The Teacher Training Agency (TTA), OfSTED and The Higher Education Funding Council of England (HEFCE). Check out Simkins if you want to read more about this.'

'But organisations could have resisted.'

'Many did. However, managers quickly found that failure to implement the new approaches could result in unfavourable audit or inspection reports that in time impacted on the organisation's funding. In order to deliver the required outcomes, managers had to abide by the new rules and abandon the old bureau-professional approach.'

'So despite early opposition, managerialism has become the dominant ideology in educational management.'

'Absolutely, there is now a greater emphasis on the need for effective management and leadership in schools and colleges as the means by which governmental and organisational goals may be achieved. A good example of this was the creation of the National College for School Leadership. And we are not talking just about leadership at the top of the organisation. Simkins suggests that, as workloads have increased and staff have been required to do more with reduced resources, the responsibilities of middle managers have increased and they have become directly accountable for the performance of staff under their control. In addition, many schools and colleges have seen their hierarchical structures reduced and made flatter by removing layers of management, with responsibility for the achievement of targets delegated to course teams. Often this process has been promoted as a means of empowering staff. However, for many people the reality is that they are required to take on additional responsibilities while the gap between them and the next layer of management increases.'

'I accept your general point, but not all managers have accepted managerialist values lock, stock and barrel. I can think of many teachers who remain as committed to their pupils as any 1970s teacher,' I said.

'I agree many have. But can you see that they will have had to trim their management and leadership style to reflect the external constraints they operate under.'

I nodded my head in agreement, but remained silent. I was thinking about my present boss who always puts learners first and a previous deputy I'd worked under who was always looking to introduce the latest management gimmick into the organisation because it would look good on her CV.

'Interestingly, some research has been undertaken on how management and staff have integrated the requirements of managerialism into their established values system. Gleeson and Shain found that with a few notable exceptions the conflict between lecturers and senior managers in further education has been overstated and oversimplifies the complex situation found in colleges. They explored the changing managerial cultures in further education among middle managers, but I'm sure the same process is at work in schools. They found that middle managers very often find themselves acting as the ideological buffer between staff and senior managers and have the unenviable task of translating policy into practice in such a way as to satisfy both senior management and staff.'

'I know how they feel. As a member of SMT I often have to deliver messages to staff that I am not entirely happy with but which have been agreed at governors or SMT level.'

'That's interesting. Gleeson and Shain identified three broad strategies that managers adopt. Strategy one, willing compliance, is characterised by the manager's wholehearted identification with institutional aims and objectives and the strategies used to achieve them. Such managers willingly embrace the managerialist agenda. Strategy two involves unwilling compliance and is characterised by the individual's rejection of the organisation's managerialist agenda. This can take one of two forms. Either the individual finds it impossible to relate to the new paradigm and hankers after a bygone age when bureau-professional values ruled or they believe that the institution has not gone far enough with the introduction of business management technologies. Strategy three requires...'

'You're going to tell me that strategy three is the compromise position.'

'I am, indeed. Strategy three is strategic compliance and it was this approach that was displayed by the majority of middle managers surveyed. It's characterised by the sophisticated way in which managers deal with the managerialist agenda while at the same time accommodating their commitment to older professional values such as collegiality and student support. This approach requires managers to balance the demands of the organisation with their own professional values. What sets such managers apart from willing compliers is that they do not identify strongly with the image of the organisation as promoted by the senior managers but recognise that their job requires them to "sell the party line". This act of distancing enables them to retain credibility with their staff while enacting instructions received from above. Which do you use?'

'I'm definitely a strategic complier.'

'And that says something about your leadership style and values. Even when you become a principal, it is likely that you will continue to implement new requirements from OfSTED or the government. But you will seek to limit any harm, as you see it, that they might cause to learners or staff.'

'So, just like leaders in the private sector who face constraints on their actions from public opinion, the will of the shareholders and the demands of the customer. I can never be truly independent,' I said.

'No. All education leaders operate within constraints that are considerably more limiting than those faced by their counterparts in the private sector. However, there is one way that you can extend your range of freedom. What do you think it is?'

After a moment's thought I smiled and replied, 'Be ridiculously successful. No one can argue with success.'

'Exactly. No one is going to argue with a principal if they are achieving outstanding results. A few years ago, Oxford University was told by the Higher Education Funding Council that it should change its management structures to reflect best practice in the sector. The members of the University rejected the request, pointing out that their old and creaking structures had produced, and continued to sustain, one of the two best universities in England. Nothing protects you like success. But if you fail…'

'All the pigeons come home to roost at the same time and your enemies enjoy a moment of **schadenfreude**.'

Here's a handout that compares the features of bureau-professionalism with managerialism. It's a useful summary (see page 23). Do you have any questions?

Nat's reflection

23 September

Maybe I've been lucky, but in all my time in education I've not found many senior managers who have been rabid managerialists. So I tend to agree with Gleeson and Shain that the gulf between managers and staff in education has been overstated. Hang on a minute. Am I saying that because as a senior manager I would like that to be the case, or is it actually the case? It's very difficult to be sure. Perhaps I could ask the staff. Maybe issue a short questionnaire or talk to one or two people who are never afraid to express an opinion.

I know I said I was a strategic complier but am I really? I suppose it all depends on what I'm being asked to do. Generally I think I'm probably a willing complier. Most of the policies and practices I've been asked to implement have been reasonable. Maybe that's because I've always worked in this managerialist paradigm and it feels natural to me. But there have been some policies that I've disagreed with. Where that happened I probably did try to make them as palatable to the staff and myself as I could. So in that sense I' am a strategic complier.

In the final analysis, I do believe that you have to do what is best for the organisation and the learners even if it runs counter to your own views. Yes, principals can make a stand against the latest government instruction. But two or three years down the line they are likely to find their school or college in serious difficulties because of poor OfSTED reports and either closed down or merged. That doesn't help learners or staff. Does that make me an unprincipled pragmatist?

Space for your notes

Prompts

- How many of the managerialist practices have been adopted by your organisation? Give examples.
- Which managerialist practices are emphasised the most in your school/college, e.g. financial control or the manager's right to manage? Give examples.
- Where does the pressure to apply these practices come from?

Review of tutorial

'I've read a bit about **performativity**: how's that different from managerialism?' I asked.

'I'm not entirely sure that it is all that different. You could argue that it is just a continuation of, or a part of the managerialist agenda. Reeves et al. describe it as a range of techniques used by management to influence the behaviour and outcomes achieved by either an individual or group at departmental or organisational level. But Stephen Ball suggests that it's a way of controlling educationalists by changing how they see their role.'

'So what are we talking about – mind control?' I asked half jokingly.

'Not quite, but almost. What Ball is saying is that in this new performativity-driven culture the teacher or lecturer is subject to continuous surveillance in the form of appraisals, target-setting, peer reviews, external inspection, report writing and annual reviews. Regardless of how they perceive this process, they are required to participate in it, and this leads to the situation where they judge their own performance and professional worth based upon how suc-cessful they were in meeting their targets.'

'So you are saying that subconsciously we come to identify with and internalise the values that underpin the targets, and in so doing we change the nature of our professional practice. Effectively the achievement of targets and objectives becomes more important to us than doing the best for our learners.' I stopped and thought for a moment. 'You know it sounds a bit like what happened at Staffordshire Hospital. The Inquiry into the high level of deaths and poor patient care there found that managers and staff became overly concerned with meet-ing targets and forgot that their primary responsibility was to the patients.'

'That is probably an extreme example and I think there were other factors at play as well, such as poor management and a shortage of funds but, yes, it could be used as an example,' Martin replied.

'Another example of targets being based on what can be measured and not on what is important,' I said.

'That's a really good point. The aim of performativity is to provide "objec-tive" information about the workings of the organisation through the use of a series of performance indicators. Now, according to writers such as Elliot and Reeves et al., there are three problems with that approach: first, it wrongly assumes that complex relationships between cause and effect can be reduced to a numerical value. Secondly, it is based upon the unproven assumption that there exist perfect standards against which it is possible to judge performance and, thirdly, that if something cannot be measured against such benchmarks it is either of little value or does not exist. In such a scenario, outcomes that cannot be captured by indicators are deemed unimportant. Can you see that this is particularly problematic for the bureau-professional whose professional practice is shaped by context, the client's needs, experience and professional judgement, the product of which can't be expressed as a simple numeric value?

I nodded in agreement. 'I suppose in this new environment it is the task of the leader to instil in all staff the attitudes and beliefs that go hand in hand with such a culture, the chief of which, if I understand you properly, is that staff are accountable for their performance, and their primary allegiance should be to the organisation and not to professional values or bodies.'

'Correct; it is this breakdown in professional allegiance that many suggest has led to a decrease in collegiality based upon common professional iden-tity and the construction of a new allegiance predicated upon loyalty to the organisation and its corporate culture. But remember that the extent to which this has actually happened is contested by writers such as Randle and Brady and Gleeson and Shain who argue that such claims have been overstated.'

'Well I've certainly noticed that teachers and lecturers are required to spend an increasing proportion of their time collecting data for monitoring and management purposes. And of course this becomes worse when OfSTED come calling. It's quite amusing really to watch the organisation invent a version of itself that it sells to the inspectors by engaging in a stage-managed event. I'm certain that the Inspectors know that what they are seeing is not the unvarnished reality. But they seem to go along with the charade.'

'You're probably right. We've covered quite a bit today so let me leave you with this thought. Most of the people who write against managerialism and performativity are on the left. But Mrs Thatcher's favourite economist was Fredrick Hayek. Now he was a free market liberal, and in some circles he has been blamed for managerialism and the so-called market reforms of the 1980s. The truth is he would have opposed nearly every change made, on the grounds that it curtailed the freedom of teachers, led to the control of education by an unelected cadre of technocrats and was predicated on the misguided belief that in a decentralised system it was possible for the centre to manage a complex function using returns supplied by schools.'

'Because the returns can only report those issues which can be measured?' I suggested.

'Yes, but Hayek would go further and say that it is impossible for any school manager to accurately report the reality of what is happening in her school as so much of their knowledge is tacit in nature and cannot be communicated verbally. The reason I mention Hayek is because it's always academically stronger to use a wide range of writers when evaluating a theory or policy. If you want to get a feel of what he has to say, check out Hayek's *The Road to Serfdom* or have a look at my website www.pearsoned/mcgrathandcoles.'

'OK,' I said.

'For our next session, have a look at organisational culture.'

Nat's reflection

25 September

Do we become what we do? Some Eastern religions believe that we do. They argue that what we do is more important than what we say we believe because actions become internalised and change beliefs. I suppose if you are constantly told that your job is to get learners through tests or exams there is a risk that you would come to see education as an exam passing process. If you buy into that, you would cease to be a teacher that wanted to develop each learner into a rounded person.

Like a lot of this discussion on managerialism and performativity, I think there is some truth in such claims. But it's not the whole truth. Every teacher I know tries to do what's best for each learner. It's not always easy. There are competing demands on time and priorities, but I don't think that teachers have sold out to targets and objectives.

Nor do I think that there has been a complete breakdown in collegiality or whatever you want to call it. Teachers still work together and support each other. As for giving our loyalty to the organisation rather than our subject or peers, didn't teachers always try to engender in the learners a feeling of belonging to the school or college? So what's changed? Possibly it's a matter of emphasis.

I'm shattered. I should write up my notes from the tutorial but they will have to wait until tomorrow. One thing is for sure, I'm going to have to take my pre-session reading seriously. It's clear that Martin expects me to be able to discuss the issues and not just listen to him. So much for an easy ride!

Space for your notes

Prompts

- What are the educational aims that you have for your learners?
- Are these aims assisted or hampered by managerialism/performativity?

Record of tutorial

Summary notes from tutorial held on 22 September

- There never was a golden age of collegiality or bureau-professionalism.
- Essentially, bureau-professionalism was based on shared values and professional ties that bound education manager, leaders and staff together. They had been socialised into the teaching profession and therefore shared common attitudes, beliefs and philosophy.
- Managerialism has been given various names including New Public Management, New Managerialism, Entrepreneurial Governance and Neo-Taylorism.
- Managerialism is based on two principles: universalism and isomorphism. Universalism suggests that all organisations should follow the structure of private for-profit organisations. Isomorphism suggests that the structure of private organisations is most efficient.
- One difficulty faced by proponents of using private sector management techniques in the public sector is that the measure of success in the public sector is votes gained at elections, not profits made.

- Value for money comprises of economy, efficiency and effectiveness.
- Managerialism is an ideology composed of a range of practices, including: emphasising the manager's right to manage, the creation of cost centres, budgetary control, breaking the organisation down into subunits that 'buy and sell' services from each other, the weakening of trade union and professional ties, and the use of VFM.
- Managerialism focuses on individual organisations, which is what makes it more effective than many previous policies targeted at the public sector.
- The introduction of managerialism led to a greater emphasis being placed on management and leadership as these skills were necessary to meet the new requirements.
- The clash between managers wedded to the new managerialist regime and staff that still hanker after the old bureau-professional settlement has been overstated.
- There is evidence that managers and staff can be divided into three categories when analysing the extent to which they have embraced managerialism, namely: willing compliers, unwilling compliers and strategic compliers.
- Managerialism does place restrictions on the leader's freedom of action.
- It's debatable if performativity is different from managerialism or a part of it. If performativity is intended to change how people think and act, then there is a case for recognising it as a separate process. The question is: to what extent have managers and teachers internalised managerialist and performative values?
- Performativity targets assume that
  - there is a relationship between cause and effect,
  - this complex relationship can be captured in a single figure,
  - there exists a set of perfect standards and
  - information which cannot be measured is unimportant.

  All four assumptions can be challenged.
- The liberal economist Fredrick Hayek would agree with many of the left's criticisms of managerialism and performativity. Where he would disagree is that the left believe in central control and he did not.

Implications of learning for my leadership style

OK, this is the important bit. How does what I have learnt impact on my leadership style?

I think I came to terms with the fact many years ago that even when I reach the top I won't be able to operate free from external restrictions. But it's disappointing to have it confirmed by Martin. I will have to take into account the dictates of policy makers and the views of others and any other constraining factors if I want to be an effective leader. Some of these are obvious, such as the views of governors and other **stakeholders**. I'll have to take the staff, learners and parents with me if I want to substantially change things. And that's even before I start to consider the general public, local authorities and the government as represented by OfSTED.

Of course some groups are more powerful than others. Even the most supine governing body has the power to stop me if they don't like what I'm doing, and OfSTED wield an enormous influence over any school or college. A series of poor OFSTED reports and I'd be shown the door. As for parents, well, they can always remove their children if they don't like the direction I'm taking – but few would. But is it ethical for me to rely on parents' inertia to get my own way? Shouldn't I try to convince them of the value of what I'm doing?

I suppose the same thing applies to staff and learners. As leader I could impose my views but that isn't likely to lead to good working relationships. No. I have to convince people to follow me willingly. If I force them to do as they are told, they will do it for a time. But they will also wait for just the right moment, when I'm exposed and at my weakest, to remove their support from me and then I'll be up the creek without a paddle or a friend.

I need to be a 'strategic complier', working within the constraints I face while doing my best to stay true to my vision of education. I have to accept that sometimes I'll have to take a step back and concede ground on an issue if it will help me to achieve my objectives further down the road.

As for performativity, that does concern me. The idea that by 'playing the targets game' a teacher could somehow morph into a number cruncher is worrying. No one ever became a teacher because they wanted to spend their lives monitoring staff and filling out statistical returns. They became a teacher in order to work with learners, to help them develop and grow, and to make a difference to their lives. It will be a sad day for teaching if we ever forget that.

So in terms of my leadership style I must share with staff my commitment to teaching and learning. They need to know that if we do our jobs as well as we can, with passion and professionalism, that we will achieve our objectives and satisfy any performative targets imposed on us.

I've ordered Hayek's *The Road to Serfdom.* I've always been interested in tacit knowledge but I've never heard of Hayek. Yet Martin tells me that he wrote *The Road* in the 1940s which is about 30 years before tacit knowledge entered mainstream education training. It will be interesting to see if he has anything new (or should that be old) to say about the subject.

Space for your notes

Prompts

● In this, and subsequent tutorials, you may want to think about how what you have learned will influence your leadership style. If you intend to do this then use the reflection at the end of each tutorial headed 'Implications of learning for my leadership style' as a template for your own reflection.

Note we have not provided space for this activity as you might easily write 2 or more pages on a chapter.

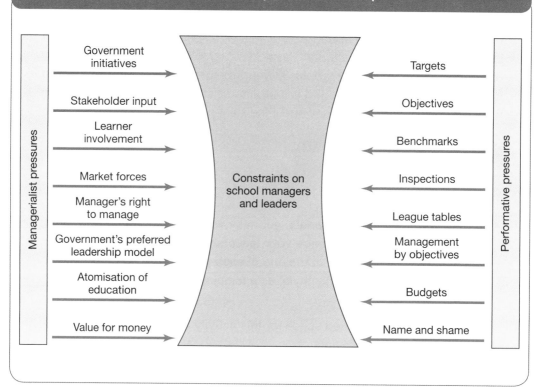

Figure 1.1 The influence exerted on educational leaders by managerialist and performative pressures

Handout

Bureau-professional accord prior to 1979	Managerialism, post 1979
Concern for the students' learning and well-being.	Practice of elevating the process of management above that which is to be managed.
Belief that lecturers should be seen as a source of expertise.	Practice of emphasising the manager's right to manage.
Loyalty to colleagues and a concern for academic standards.	Use of cost centres and devolved budgets to achieve greater financial control.
Commitment to public service, with the needs and rights of students paramount.	Extensive use of performance indicators in order to monitor and control staff activities.
Belief that quality of provision should be assessed on the basis of inputs.	Application of VFM principles in order to ensure economy, efficiency and effectiveness, and the monitoring of organisations at the institutional level.
Belief that resources should be deployed on the basis of educational need.	Creation of a quasi-market environment that promotes competition and transforms students into customers.
Belief that, because managers were socialised within a particular profession or discipline, they should share the same values as their staff.	Atomisation of large-scale organisations into subunits that are viewed as chains of low-trust relationships linked only by contracts.
Belief that, as managers and lecturers shared similar professional backgrounds and socialisation, their relationship should be one based on mutual trust, a respect for professional autonomy and recognition that accountability should be to peers, not managers.	Weakening of trade union and professional ties within the workplace as a prelude to the creation of a more flexible workforce, and the introduction of appraisal systems and performance-related pay as a means of aligning the individual's aims and objectives more closely with those of the organisation.

(List adapted from Dunleavy and Hood, 1994; Prichard, 1996; Power, 1997; Randle and Brady, 1997; Deem, 1998; Trowler, 1998; Simkins, 1999).

Additional information on the issues covered by this tutorial can be found at/in:

- www.pearsoned.com/mcgrathandcoles

- **Ball, S.J.** (2002) *The Teacher's Soul and the Terrors of Performativity.* www.ioe.ac.uk/rss/professorstephenball.htm.

- **Gleeson, D. and Shain, F.** (1999) Managing ambiguity: between markets and managerialism – a case study of 'middle' managers in further education, *Sociological Review*, 47(3): 461–90.

- **Olssen, M. and Peters, M.A.** (2005) Neo-liberalism, higher education and the knowledge economy: from the free market to knowledge capitalism, in *The Journal of Education Policy*, 20(3): 313–43.

Tutorial 2

Organisational culture

Aim of tutorial

By the end of this tutorial you will be able to analyse the organisational culture that you operate within and understand the constraints that it imposes on your choice of leadership style.

Contents

- Towards a definition of organisational culture
- The role of principals in changing/maintaining organisational culture
- Handy's four organisational cultures – role, bureaucratic, task and person
- Mapping the culture in your organisation
- Hargreaves – Balkanised cultures
- Johnson and Scholes – defender and prospector cultures
- Deal and Kennedy – risk averse culture
- Morgan – organisational culture as metaphors

Nat's reflection

29 September

Well, it was pretty clear from our first meeting that Martin wants our meeting to be a dialogue rather than him teaching and me listening. So I've done some revision for this session by rereading Charles Handy's ideas on organisational culture. I found the info on www.businessballs.com. It covers training and general management issues and I think it's going to be a very useful source of info. Although I expect that Martin will want me to read more widely.

Review of tutorial

Martin was sitting at his desk, hands crossed in his lap when I entered. He reminded me of a statue of the Buddha that I had seen at the British Museum. Turning he smiled and said, '**Back again?**'

'I had nowhere else to go,' I joked and sat down.

Martin smiled, turned over a piece of paper headed Nat Lang and said, 'Last time we looked at managerialism, which is a significant part of the external culture in which schools and colleges operate. Today I want to look at organisational culture, which is the internal environment within an organisation. How would you define organisational culture?'

Having seen how Martin operated during the first session I'd done a bit more preparatory reading and was able to respond confidently: 'I'm not sure I can define it but I'd describe it as the basic assumptions, beliefs, expectations, norms and values that are shared by the members of the organisation. In turn these assumptions have been influenced by the organisation's history, rituals, routines, organisational structure, purposes, and traditions. Most importantly, it operates at an unconscious level to define the organisation's view of itself and provides guidance for decision makers even though they are unaware of its influence. In simplistic terms I think of it as the organisation's personality and, as such, it defines how people in the organisation think and act.'

'You've been doing some reading,' Martin said smiling. '**Charles Handy argues that it's impossible to define a culture precisely. He says it's something that is felt and only vaguely perceived. But Johnson and Scholes try to define it. They suggest that it's composed of the organisation's stories, myths, rituals symbols, leadership and management styles and structures and systems. Mind you, given that it's multifaceted, organic and constantly evolving, it's hardly surprising that it is difficult to define organisational culture in concise terms.**'

'If it's organic I take it that it can't be imposed on an organisation. It has to grow naturally,' I said.

'**I'd agree to some extent. It is something that grows and, if damaged or destroyed, it's difficult to replace. But it's also sensitive to change and therefore responds to both external and internal pressures. I like to think of it as a compost bin and everything gets thrown into it and composts down. Now, good compost can nourish a garden but if it's too strong it will scorch and kill the plants. Some writers such as Bennis and Nanus, and Schein argue that a leader's most important function is to maintain or change the organisation's culture as required. But they have to get it right or face real problems.**'

'I would have thought that where an organisation's culture was well established, as in most schools and colleges, it would be wisest to work with the culture than to work against it and try to establish a new one.'

'**You might be right. When further education colleges became independent from local authority control in 1992/3, a number of colleges appointed principals from the private sector, but by 1996/7 most had left. It's said that they couldn't come to terms with the culture of FE.**'

'Why didn't they change it? They had the power,' I said.

'**Often, leaders have the most power when their organisation is either doing very well or very badly.**'

'Because if they are doing well they get the credit, and if the organisation is in a bad way people look to them to solve their problems.'

'**Precisely, now most colleges were doing OK immediately after incorporation in 1993 and up to 1995. Things were ticking over nicely. So, many managers saw no reason to change. It was only from 1996 onwards when the new funding methodology really started to bite that things started to get difficult for many colleges.**'

'And by then the principals had left,' I said. Martin nodded in agreement and I continued. 'But in the private sector when a new managing director is appointed she often gets rid of the old senior management team. That exercise of power demonstrates to everyone that they are in charge and it gives them the freedom to implement their ideas and change the culture. Why didn't the new principals do that?' I asked.

'Perhaps because they did not understand how FE worked and needed experienced FE managers around them. Perhaps because the college governors or even the senior managers' contracts of employment made it too difficult or expensive to get rid of them.'

'OK, so some find they can't operate in a particular culture and leave but any new leader who stays must have some effect on the culture,' I said. 'I mean they have the power to make an impression.'

'They do indeed. I think it's true to say that whether a principal remakes or just interprets an organisation's culture it will always reflect to some extent their beliefs, personality and views.'

Martin could see that I was trying to turn into words a vague thought that was floating at the back of my mind and remained silent. Something I'd read. What was it? Finally I said, 'I suppose that the principal has the greatest direct influence over those he works most with – the senior management team. So would I be right in thinking that they act like carriers of the new or changed culture to the rest of the staff?'

'Actually Southworth found a lot of evidence to suggest that this is exactly what happens. As we will see when we talk about Handy's Power Culture, **senior managers often mimic the behaviour and attitudes of the principal. This process of identification and adoption means that changes in organisational culture usually only occurs when there is a change of** CEO **or in senior management.'**

'So we come back to the fact that new principals very often get rid of the previous senior management team in order to recruit people who are sympathetic to their ideas and amenable to cultural change?'

'They may do that if they think that the SMT **is a barrier to change.'**

Nat's reflection

29 September

In my last school a new principal was appointed and it was obvious from her first day on the job that she was determined to wipe out any memory of the previous principal. She made it very clear to the deputies and assistant principals that she wanted us out. It was her first principalship and I wondered, at the time, if she saw us as a threat to her authority. But maybe she just wanted to change things and saw us as an impediment.

If she wanted to change the school's culture she may have calculated that the quickest way to do that was to change those that helped carry the culture to the staff. Mind you it didn't work out too well for her. We left and the people she appointed weren't up to the job and two years down the line the school was in special measures. She probably acted too hastily. She should have spent more time sizing up the school and working out who in the management team she could work with and who needed to be moved on. Her 'scorched earth policy' resulted in too many new managers who did not understand the school, its teachers, students or parents. Which is another way of saying that the school's organisational culture 'did for her'.

Martin seemed obsessed with the idea of defining organisational culture. I suppose it's what academic do – name and define things. I'm not going to get too hung up on it. I like my idea that organisational culture can be thought of as the organisation's personality. And just as you have to take into account an individual's personality when dealing with them on a sensitive issue, you have to understand your 'school's personality' when you are trying to exercise leadership or bring about a change. Hang on, does personality cover it? What I've just written implies that I have to be concerned about how the person or organisation reacts. So is it better to think of organisational culture as both the personality of the organisation and how it acts and reacts to events both mundane and unusual? That's something worth thinking about.

Space for your notes

Prompts

● Describe your school or college's organisational culture in 30 words or less.

● To what extent does your organisation reflect the attitudes, beliefs and values of the chief executive or senior management team? Give examples.

Review of tutorial

'Now there are numerous models of organisational culture but some are more useful for the busy deputy or department head than others and it's those that I want to concentrate on,' Martin said. 'Handy developed one of the most popular theories when he suggested that an organisation's culture is formed by the unique combination of four archetypal cultures namely: **club**, **role**, **task** and **person**. Are you familiar with his ideas?'

'Yes. At one time it seemed that every management course I went on covered Handy's "Gods of Management Theory" and I skim read it again for this session.'

'Good, so you can tell me what it's all about then.'

Me and my big mouth, why didn't I just keep quiet? 'Well, one thing Handy stressed was that it is was highly unlikely that you would find only one of his archetypal cultures in an organisation. Instead, there would be elements of two or more with perhaps one being dominant. The precise mix would depend on the organisation's size, type of work, environment and history. So, for example, in one school you might find a power culture where the principal is very much in charge and power is exercised through a role culture with bits of task culture represented by project groups and the person culture championed by a few individuals in the organisation.'

'Good but you know what I'm going to ask next?'

'You want me to describe each culture.'

'Exactly.'

'OK. A club or power culture exists when there is one central power source. The power source can be an individual or a small group of like-minded individuals, such as the SMT. Power and influence radiate from this central source and are communicated to the various departments. Handy likens this culture to that of a spider's web, where any movement by the spider at the centre reverberates to all parts of the web and causes staff to react.'

'This "causing staff to react" is important,' Martin said. 'Power or club cultures rely on precedent, on anticipating the wishes and decisions of the central power source. Management teams often seek to mimic and/or anticipate the actions of the chief executive. In genuine power cultures there are few rules or procedures and very little bureaucracy with the result that the "power source" is free to act as they please.'

'So in such cases the principal selects her management team on the basis that they share her attitudes and beliefs.'

'Exactly. Leaders who encourage a power culture place great trust in individuals and very little in committees. In a power culture the leader and the SMT is concerned with outcomes and, provided a person delivers, they aren't too worried about how you achieved it. Such organisations are essentially political in nature. By that I mean that decisions are taken on the basis of the balance of influence rather than by following a set of procedures or rules. So whichever faction has the most credibility or influence with the leader at any particular time will usually see their advice accepted.'

'It reminds me of a programme I saw about Hitler. Everyone thinks that the Nazis were highly organised and systematic. But Hitler used to hold long dinners in the evening at which many of the Nazi hierarchy were present. He would ramble on for hours about his vision for Germany. Based upon what he said, those present would try to work out what would please him and then take action. It was their way of gaining favour and advancement.'

'I think I saw the same programme. Hitler believed in the survival of the fittest. He wanted his subordinates to compete with each other to win his approval.

He believed that this was an effective way to govern a county – which was one reason he failed. Thank goodness. OK, what do you know about role cultures?'

'A role culture is basically a **bureaucracy**. Handy likens it to a Greek temple where the specialist departments are the pillars of the structure and a small executive at the top forms the pediment linking all the departments together. In such cultures the work of the departments and the interactions between them are tightly prescribed by rules, written procedures and regulations and the role a person plays is more important than the individual who fills it…'

Martin interrupted my flow, observing that **'Years ago I used to work at the Department for Education and painted on every office door was the title of the occupant, for example Assistant Secretary. But the name of the person filling that role was on a piece of wood that could be slid in and out of a holder above the title.'**

'I suppose it was to remind every civil servant that they were replaceable,' I said.

'Ooh happy days!' said Martin with a smile. **'In addition every employee was selected on the basis that they could satisfactorily perform the specified role. Performance over and above that prescribed in your job description was frowned upon because it could clash with someone else's role. So you can see that in a bureaucracy positional power dominates and the exercise of personal power is curtailed.'**

'But schools very often have a power culture running alongside a powerful bureaucracy. How does that work?' I asked.

'The key word you used was mixture. Genuine power cultures typically exist in organisations run by the founder/owner. It's her baby. She can do with it whatever she likes. Now, while a powerful principal can dominate a school, she doesn't own it and is subject to control in various forms by the school governors, OfSTED and the local authority. And while they might have a degree of personal power, their greatest source of power flows from their position.'

'It's odd, isn't it, that while schools and colleges are obviously bureaucratic they avoid using the term. It's as if bureaucracy is seen as a dirty word. But you need some bureaucracy, otherwise no one would get paid on time!'

'I agree absolutely. Bureaucracy is often used pejoratively as a synonym for inefficiency. But originally it was used to describe any organisation where the owners of the organisation were not involved in its running and where hierarchical authority and respect for the organisation's structure were paramount,' Martin said.

'But today most people think of bureaucratic organisations as impersonal and inefficient. With staff specialising in particular tasks and where they use written rules and regulations to make decisions.'

'That's true, but originally this was seen as strength because pre-written rules would ensure fairness of treatment.'

'So the principal couldn't give a place to her friend's child unless they met the prescribed criteria,' I said.

'Exactly. All decisions were transparent. In truth there is still a large element of bureaucracy in every educational organisation in the country and of course the imposition of managerialism has meant that more rules, regulations and data collection have been required...'

'Leading to more bureaucracy.'

'Which is ironic as managerialism was intended to reduce bureaucracy, with managers empowered to make decisions. But the need to record results and follow centrally imposed policies has seen an increase in bureaucracy. Hardly a day goes by without the *Daily Mail* running a story about the number of police hours wasted on form filling when they should be out catching criminals.'

'The **law of unintended consequences**,' I said.

Martin groaned at the pun. '**Exactly, which is another reason why it is absurd for some writers on managerialism and performativiy to claim that it was inspired by the work of Hayek. He knew the dangers of unintended consequences.**'

'You seem to be a fan of Hayek. Are you, or have you ever been the lone right wing academic in the Faculty of Education?' I demanded in my best Joseph McCarty imitation.

'Hardly. I'm middle of the road. That's why I get run over by traffic going in both directions. No, I'm just keen that students read both sides of an argument before making up their mind. As Hayek once said, good academic work involves presenting your opponent's strongest possible arguments before you try to dismantle them.'

'Rob Lowe said something similar in an episode of *The West Wing*.'

'A fellow Wingnut! What's your favourite episode?'

'*The Supremes*, Season 5,' I said without hesitation. 'What's yours?'

'*In the Shadow of the Gunman Parts 1 and 2*, Season 2. We'll have to have a chat sometime. But let's get back to business.'

'OK, where was I?' I said. 'Oh yes, while I accept what you say about the power and role cultures, I have noticed that many schools encourage a sort of task culture. Where attempts are made to bring together the staff and other resources required to complete a specific task. Many teachers like this approach.'

'That's true. From experience I would say that most teachers like to work in this collaborative way. Handy represented the approach as a net because of the way various stands/people are woven together to form a team. In such "task groups" expert knowledge is highly regarded and individual objectives, status and style are set aside as the needs of the team are paramount. Such a culture is highly adaptable and can act quickly when required as each team contains the expertise, resources and power to make decisions and implement them. But management can be wary of such groups because they can be difficult to control, as day-to-day management of the project resides with the team.'

'So in a way it's a throwback to collegiality?'

'Perhaps. Collegiality does attempt to draw on expertise from all parts of the organisation in order to maximise the effectiveness of decision making. But, unlike genuine collegial working, the powers and remit of the team are very clearly prescribed by senior management and they retain overall control by deciding which projects will be resourced and crucially when the team will be disbanded.'

'So what would be the features of a truly collegial organisation?' I asked.

'The notion that a collegial approach is the most appropriate way to run an educational organisation has, according to Bush, entered into folklore. As I intimated in the last tutorial, there never was a golden age of collegiality where power was shared among some or all the members of the organisation, and organisational policy and decision making were the product of discussion leading to consensus.'

'So why do we continue to hear about it in schools and colleges?'

'Possibly because it is democratic and suggests that management should be based upon agreement. It's also an approach that is particularly suited to organisations that contain a high number of professionals …'

'Because part of being a professional is that you are free to exercise your professional judgement as to how best to deal with a situation,' I said.

'Exactly. OK, on to the last of Handy's cultures – the person culture. Although such cultures rarely exist, it is not uncommon to find one or two individuals who believe that the organisation exists purely to assist them in their work. This can be the source of considerable conflict if the dominant culture is different.'

'So why are they allowed to persist with such behaviour?' I asked.

'**Sometimes sorting them out can be more trouble than it's worth and most teachers and students have a soft spot for the odd eccentric.**'

'I've got to admit there has been one in every organisation I ever worked in. And by and large people liked them. They were different. They added a little spice to organisational life. But I can't think of any organisation that would want more than a few on the payroll.'

'**What about an architects' practice where a group of professionals come together, rent premises and hire administrative staff in order to practise their profession? The organisational structure would be minimal and focus on the needs of the architects, and management control mechanisms would only operate with the consent of the individuals. And of course professional expertise would be the source of the greatest power.**'

'I suppose barristers' chambers would be similar but you could also describe such organisations as power cultures!' I said.

'**That's an interesting thought. Where does one begin and the other end?**'

Nat's reflection

30 September

I have to admit that ever since I came across it I've had a soft spot for Handy's model of organisational culture. It's practical and easy to apply. All you have to do is observe what is going on in your organisation and try to categorise actions and events into one of his four categories. I usually do it my head, but maybe next time I move jobs I should keep a reflective diary. I could jot down significant events and how they are dealt with and use that data to identify the cultural factor at play. Using a journal might speed up the process and make it more accurate.

➡

Thinking about the jobs I've had over the years, I can see that I have been most successful in role and task cultures and I quite like having a few eccentrics about – but I can't stand power cultures. They are so unpredictable and arbitrary. I don't like having to jump at the whim of a spider at the centre of the web. Somehow it feels demeaning and sycophantic. I'd never make a good courtier. Is it any wonder that I have avoided working for any principal who thinks that the organisation is theirs to do with as they like?

As for bureaucratic organisations, I can put up with a fair level of bureaucracy, provided that the systems and rules aren't seen as more important than the function of educating young people. Besides, every organisation needs a certain level of bureaucracy in order to function – even if it's just to pay the wages. Without it, chaos would ensue.

As for collegiality, I'm not sure I do hanker after it. Trying to arrive at a consensus on anything from a group of teachers or lecturers is like herding cats. Decision making would take forever. No, consultation has to be the way forward. You consult staff, take into account what they have to say and then make your decision on the basis of what is in the best interests of the organisation as you honestly see it.

But consultation has to be real and genuine. Not as in the case of one principal I worked for who wanted to change the name of the college. He asked staff and students to choose a new name from a list of four. We were told that 48 per cent of staff and students had voted for the name finally chosen. The only problem was that I couldn't find anyone who had opted for that choice. The fix was confirmed when, within a week of announcing the winning name, all the signs in the college were replaced with nice new shiny plaques which must have taken weeks to produce.

Space for your notes

Prompts

- Using Handy's four archetypes describe your organisation's culture.
- How collegial is your organisation? What part does staff play in the decision-making process? Give examples to support your answers.

Review of tutorial

'So far you've implied that an organisation has a single culture made up of four features. But I've seen schools where there is more than one distinct culture at play. How does that work?' I asked.

'You're talking about Hargreaves and his Balkanised cultures. What happens is that while the organisation will have a single distinct culture it will also have specific subcultures within a department, faculty, subject area or location. Such Balkanised cultures have certain characteristics. Each subgroup is a separate entity just like the many countries of the Balkans and there is "low permeability" between the groups. Which means that they erect "walls" to keep out the influence of other cultures; once these barriers have been erected, it is difficult to remove them. People become attached to and identify with their subgroup and over time develop a set of self-interests that they actively promote even when they conflict with the good of the whole organisation.'

'So a leader would have to sort that out.'

'Definitely. While a degree of competition between subgroups can build *esprit de corps* and improve performance, you can't allow it to harm the overall well-being of the organisation. Think about the British Army. Every regiment has its own traditions and culture and they are encouraged to think of themselves as the best. But in time of war they have to work in harmony with other units.'

'What about Johnson and Scholes. Did they develop a theory to go with their definition?'

'Indeed they did. They suggested a number of questions that a researcher might ask when exploring organisational culture, including: What kind of behaviour is expected and rewarded by the organisation? Is risk taking encouraged or discouraged? What types of strategy are favoured by the organisation, defensive or speculative? By asking such questions and examining corporate strategies, past decisions and organisational systems, they believed a researcher could distinguish between what they called prospector and defender organisations.'

'Let me guess,' I said. 'Prospector organisations take risks while defender organisations dislike risk and are concerned with maintaining stability.'

'Ah, Mr Poirot, your little grey cells are working well today,' Martin said. 'Prospector organisations expand through product and market development and emphasise the need for flexibility by decentralising management control. For example, in schools many of the early applicants for Academy status probably fall into the prospector category. Defender organisations seek to protect their current position and grow cautiously by improving economy and efficiency. They aren't trail blazers but they are interested in improving their performance. Organisational control is centralised, and extensive use is made of formal planning.'

'So I could use Johnson and Scholes' ideas to expand Handy's analysis. For example, a power culture could either court risk or be risk adverse, depending on the preferences of the central power source. Similarly, while a role culture would usually be risk adverse, it might pursue high-risk strategies if the senior management team were so inclined and circumstances permit.'

'You've got it!'

'What other models are there?'

'There are several others. For example, Deal and Kennedy suggest that in many public sector organisations employees receive very little feedback from stakeholders or managers until something goes wrong. This means that staff are reluctant to take any action without express approval from their line manager and seldom ask themselves if the task is worth doing or could be done in a different way.'

'Because they are only concerned with completing the task according to the "book".'

'Exactly. Then there is Schein's model which uses a three-tier model to examine the organisation's culture through its artefacts, espoused values and basic underlying assumptions. And finally I'd mention Morgan's description of organisational culture in terms of eight metaphors.'

'Eight metaphors?'

'Yes, he uses eight different metaphors to describe an organisation's culture. For example, you can think of the culture as a machine, a living organism, a set of cultures, a brain, a political system, a psychic prison, a vehicle for domination or as a system that is in constant flux and transformation.'

'Both Schein and Morgan's theories sound complicated,' I said.

'They provide a different way of thinking about an organisation's culture and are worth looking at. Both seek to present a more detailed picture of an organisation's culture than Handy's model and therefore are more difficult to apply.'

'I think I'll stick with Handy, Hargreaves, and Johnson and Scholes. Any teacher could use them either singly or in combination to dig into the culture of their school or college. They don't require a lot of training or expertise; you just have to reflect on the organisation you work in and very quickly you will be able to see aspects of these theories at work.'

'Fair enough. For next time, have a look at the difference between management and leadership and, while you are at it, look at power, what it is and where it comes from. OK?'

'Fine.'

Nat's reflection

01 October

I like the idea of using Handy's theory as the basis for analysing the organisation's culture and then using Johnson and Scholes' Prospector and Defender theory to give it an additional dimension. If I then throw in Hargreaves' ideas on Balkanised cultures, I can develop a fairly detailed picture of the culture I'm working in. But I'll definitely need to keep a reflective journal if I'm going to drill down into the culture. There is too much detail to keep it all in my head.

Hang on a minute. If I'm a new principal, people will expect me to meet with them and ask questions. I could use those meetings as a way of collecting information on the organisation's culture from a range of people. That would provide me with much better data than just relying on my own observations. I can feel a small-scale informal piece of research coming on. I'd better lie down before I feel compelled to act on it.

Space for your notes

Prompts

- Do you think that the senior managers in your workplace created the organisation's culture or simply worked with the culture already in place?
- Give examples of how your organisation's culture informs the actions of staff and management.

Record of tutorial

Summary notes from tutorial held on 29 September

Organisational culture

- Despite the efforts of many writers, there is no agreed definition of organisational culture.
- In general terms, organisational culture results from the history, rituals, routines, organisational aims, structures, management style, purposes and traditions of the organisation. These combine to influence how people think, act and behave in the organisation.
- Organisation culture is organic. It can't be imposed but is sensitive to both internal and external influence/pressure.
- The mix of factors that go to make up organisational culture can be envisaged as the weeds and leaves that form a compost heap. They rot down and form a mulch that can either nourish or harm the plants.
- Many writers believe that a leader's most important task is to either maintain or change organisational culture depending on what is required.
- Organisational culture will always reflect, to some extent, the leader's attitudes, beliefs and values.
- Leaders can create or maintain organisational culture; deputies and managers carry and spread it to staff.
- There are numerous models of organisational culture. One of the most popular and easy to use is Handy's 'Gods of Management Model'.
- Handy's model suggests that all organisational cultures are a combination of the following four: Club/power, Role/bureaucracy, Team/task and Personal/existentialist.
- A club/power culture exists when there is one central power source. Staff base their actions and decisions on what they think will please the person or group that exercises power.
- A role culture exists when detailed instructions and procedures are used to determine how individuals should act and/or make decisions.
- A task culture exists when staff work in teams to achieve a specified objective.
- A personal culture exists when an organisation exists solely to help the individual exercise their skills and expertise. For example, in architects' practices and barristers' chambers.
- Every organisation needs an element of bureaucracy to survive.

- When studying any subject it is essential that you consider both sides of every argument. When you find a writer that you disagree with, present their strongest arguments before you attempt to disprove their argument.
- True collegiality requires consensus on both the aims and objectives of an organisation among staff and similar consensus on all decisions made. This is virtually impossible to achieve and is hugely time-consuming. Genuine consultation on significant issues is a workable alternative.
- Within any school or college there can exist distinct subcultures based upon departments, teams, subject areas or houses.
- Johnson and Scholes' theory can be applied to education. Schools and colleges can be described as either prospector or defender organisations, depending on the level of risk they are willing to tolerate.
- Deal and Kennedy's theory suggests that the type of management displayed in the public sector, where staff are seldom praised for good work but regularly criticised for mistakes, leads to a culture of defensiveness and an unwillingness to act without express instructions from management.
- Morgan's eight metaphors: which include that of a machine, a living organism, a set of cultures, a brain, a political system, a psychic prison, a vehicle for domination or a system that is in constant flux and transformation.
- Theories can be combined to help analyse and provide a more detailed analysis of an organisation's culture.

Implications of learning for my leadership style

As a member of a senior management team I have to recognise that I am not the originator of the organisational culture. I'm a carrier. It's my job to carry it to staff and pupils.

When I finally do become principal, I will need to analyse the organisation's culture. If the school is doing well, then I have the choice of leaving well enough alone, but if we are in difficulty I will have to act decisively to change things. That means I have to be prepared to push through my vision for the school and anyone who does not want to hitch their star to my wagon will have to go. Am I really that ruthless? Would I be willing to sack one or more people if I thought it was in the best interest of the school, or to make their lives so uncomfortable that they would leave? If I'm not, then maybe principalship is not for me. I need to seriously think about this. What was it that Napoleon said – 'To lead is to decide'.

So what type of culture would I like to build? I don't like power cultures so I would need to avoid becoming the spider at the centre of the web. Some bureaucracy is essential so I would want very clear guidelines, instructions and procedures for key tasks. But I don't want every little part of school life bureaucratised. So keep it to the essentials. I do want to encourage team working and I'm happy to consult with people, but I and SMT would be responsible for making the final decision even if it was unpopular.

It sounds like I want to be a leader that runs a well-organised school, where people are free to express their views but are then required to implement whatever decisions I and the senior management team make.

There is only one problem with these musings: my ability to change the organisation's culture will depend to a large degree on my own personal power and influence and how ingrained the culture is. If I am perceived as weak, then I may find it very difficult or even impossible to change the culture. If that happens I may have to change my leadership style.

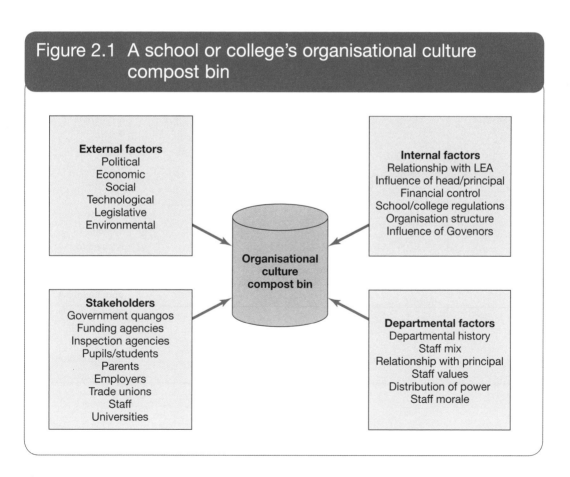

Figure 2.1 A school or college's organisational culture compost bin

Handout

Table 2.1 A comparison of six theories on organisational culture

Theorist	Culture as … A set of characteristics	Culture as … An attitude of mind	Culture as … A series of dispersed entities	Culture as … As anthropology	Culture as … A sociological metaphor
Handy	Power, bureaucracy, task or individual				
Johnson and Scholes		Defender or prospector			
Hargreaves			Balkanised cultures		
Schein				Artefacts Underlying assumptions Espoused values	
Deal and Kennedy		Risk averse			
Morgan					A machine A living organism A set of cultures A brain A political system, A psychic prison, A vehicle for domination, A system that is in constant flux and transformation.

Additional information on the issues covered by this tutorial can be found at/in:

- www.pearsoned.com/mcgrathandcoles
- www.businessballs.com
- **Cole, G.A.** (2004) *Management Theory and Practice*, (6th edn). London: Thompson.
- **Handy, C.** (1991) *Gods of Management.* London: Century Business.

Management, leadership and power

Aim of tutorial

By the end of the tutorial you will be able to critically evaluate whether there is a significant difference between management and leadership, explain why education leadership is different from leadership in a commercial organisation and list the sources of power available to a principal.

Contents

- Defining management and leadership
- Why has leadership replaced administration and management as the privileged term used to describe what principals do?
- The distinguishing features of managers and leaders
- Why education leadership is different from leadership in other sectors
- The sources of power

06 October

Well, today it's all about the difference between management and leadership – if there is any. I've always found it very difficult to decide whether an action should be categorised as management or leadership. Take motivation, for example. If you motivate someone to achieve their targets, is that management or leadership? Academics do like to analyse and define the life out of concepts, while most teachers are far too busy to think about such esoteric nonsense. Still, I wonder what spin Martin will put on it. Hopefully he will have something more profound to say than 'Managers do things right and leaders do the right things' which was the basis of one very expensive leadership seminar I went on.

Review of tutorial

Martin was rifling in his briefcase when I arrived. Straightening up, he handed me a framed photograph of *The West Wing* cast standing in front of a giant American flag. '**I thought you might like to see it,**' he said '**It's been signed by Martin Sheen, Allison Janney and Dulé Hill.**'

I took the photo and held it like a holy relic. 'That's great. Where did you get it?'

'**The wonders of the internet. I picked it up from a website that specialises in TV memorabilia.**'

I resisted the temptation to run from the room holding my trophy aloft and reluctantly handed it back saying, 'It's a beauty.'

Martin propped the photo up on his desk and said, '**OK, management and leadership. You've had a chance to read up on them. How would you define them?**' Martin sat back smiling, knowing that he had asked a really tough question.

'You're not a very nice man, are you?' I said. His smile grew broader. 'OK, here goes. Years ago Drucker said that managers do five things: they set objectives;

organise resources, including people; motivate and communicate with staff; measure results and develop people, including themselves.'

'OK, so you have defined management in terms of what a manager does.'

'Yes.'

'What about leadership?' asked Martin.

'Well, it's about influencing a group or an individual to achieve a specific objective.'

'So, again, you are defining leadership in terms of what a leader does. Can you see any overlap between the two functions? '

'There are several,' I said. 'I mean you could say that, in order to influence a group to achieve a common objective, a leader has to set objectives, organise, motivate and communicate with the group and measure progress and develop people's abilities.'

'I agree. In fact, I'd go so far as to argue that trying to differentiate management from leadership may not be necessary or worthwhile because, first, the vast majority of managerial posts contain elements of both leadership and management, and holders do not consciously differentiate between the two processes. Secondly, what followers recognise as management or leadership may differ, depending upon time, place and context.'

'I understand the first point, but can you give me an example of the second?'

'Years ago I was working in the Department for Education. We had our first ever computers delivered early in May and loaded all the data on to the new machines from paper records. Then over the Bank Holiday we were burgled and the whole office was trashed. The staff were really down. All that work gone to waste. But suddenly the department manager appeared, rolled up his sleeves and got stuck in. Now, the manager was only one step removed from God and his arrival really galvanised the staff. He didn't stay more than an hour, but it was a genuine act of leadership even though the work he did was manual and administrative.'

'What you're saying is that the context made it an act of leadership and the staff recognised the symbolic nature of what the manager had done.'

'Precisely. Now a lot of writers, including Gronn, are dubious of the value of distinguishing management from leadership. He asks when it was that commentators started to give certain words such as "leader" and "leading" a privileged status and relegate previously privileged words such as "manager"

and "management" to the role of villain, and he disputes the view that resource management does not involve leadership.'

'I find it surprising that management has been downgraded. I think that efficient management is always required if the leader's vision is to be realised in the classroom and wider organisation. I mean someone has to implement it,' I said.

'Very true. But fashions change and academics are always trying to re-categorise and differentiate phenomena; it's one way of building a reputation. For example, in the 1960s all the talk was about efficient administration in the public sector. There used to be a highly regarded postgraduate diploma available from the University of London called the Diploma in Public Administration. But by the 1980s administration was seen as reactive, stodgy and out of date. What was needed was management that was proactive, dynamic and forward looking. Then, some time in the early 90s, management fell out of favour. It was seen as staid, with managers lacking vision and only concerned with managing resources effectively rather than asking the really big questions that leaders ask, such as "Are our aims and objectives the right aims and objectives?" Yet the job of a principal has not changed that much in the past fifty years. Yes, technology has changed and they have picked up a few new duties. But essentially their main job has always been to maximise the performance of their school or college, and to do that they have to mobilise the staff.'

'So you're saying that the function hasn't changed, just the label used to describe it.'

'Yes, a case of old wine in new bottles. If you think about it, many of the principals in the 60s and 70s had served as officers during the war and knew a thing or two about how to lead. So it does annoy me when academics write about education leadership as if it is something new. What's new is the growth in the number of leadership theories, which we will get on to in the next tutorial.'

'OK, but surely with the growth in the number of theories we have some agreement on how to define leadership?'

'You'd think so, but there is very little agreement. For example, Stogdill suggests that there are almost as many definitions of leadership as there are commentators, while Warren believes that theorising the notion of academic leadership is particularly difficult as it has multiple facets and is full of paradoxes.'

'Well, if we can't compare definitions how can we distinguish between management and leadership in any discussions we have?'

'We do what you did. We look at what managers and leaders do. Here are a couple of handouts that I use (see page 62). Table 3.1 outlines the different perspectives that managers and leader have and Table 3.2 looks at the different activities that they carry out. Let's take Table 3.1 first. Does anything strike you?' Martin handed me the first table.

I looked at the table and tried to identify a pattern. The best I could come up with was, 'It looks like managers are concerned with the mundane, the day-to-day work of the organisation while leaders are dreamers, always looking to the future.'

'That's not bad. Field Marshall Lord Slim once said that management is of the mind – it's a science – while leadership is of the heart and soul and is an art. I think that's what you are seeing when you talk of the mundane and dreams. He also said that, while management was important, leadership was essential. Now what do you make of Table 3.2?' Martin asked.

'I read the table twice trying to think of something profound to say, or at least interesting, but the best I could come up with was, 'As before, the leadership column emphasises the future and change but also suggests that the leader is the face of the organisation to the wider world. In addition, you've separated out the three Es. Economy and efficiency you've given to the manager but effectiveness, setting the right targets and objectives, you've allocated to the leader. That corresponds with what you said about effectiveness being the most important of the three Es (see Tutorial 1). But I'm not sure what you mean by problem seeking.'

'Problem seeking involves scanning the horizon and trying to identify problems before they arise ...'

'And that way you can prepare for them or take action to avoid them.'

'Precisely. But I want to add one feature of leadership that is missing from both tables and that is the notion that leadership is bestowed on the individual by their followers whereas the title 'manager' often accompanies appointment to a particular post. You can't be appointed as leader even if the job title includes the word 'leader'. Followers have to see you as a leader.'

'Has anyone ever told North Korea or Burma that?'

'That's a good example. In Burma the Generals are in power but the people's leader is Aung San Suu Kyi.'

Nat's reflection

07 October

It's interesting how in the social sciences even widely used terms defy definition. I mean, in the natural sciences, the first thing a scientist does is to define their terms as precisely as possible. Therefore physicists all know and understand the differences between, say, an atom and a nucleus. I suppose it has something to do with the nature of the knowledge that they work with. For the scientist, knowledge is discoverable, hard, and real, while the social scientist is very often dealing with concepts that only exist in people's minds. And as people have different conceptions of love, beauty, democracy and leadership, it's not possible to provide a precise definition. And if you don't have precise definitions of management and leadership, it's difficult to differentiate between them. You can't even claim that leadership is something you recognise when you see it, because not everyone will recognise certain behaviours as leadership. I mean, many people in America saw George W. Bush as a strong leader after 9/11, but many others thought he was out of his depth and being manipulated by people lurking in the shadows.

Perhaps it's the nature of knowledge in the social sciences that leaves Martin dubious of the value of differentiating management from leadership. Instead, what he has done is try to look at what managers and leaders do while accepting that, depending on time, place and/or context, an act can be one of administration, management or leadership.

I do agree with Martin that you can't be appointed to the post of leader; that title has to be bestowed upon you by the staff. I remember when I was working in the local government every one accepted that the Director of Education was the person responsible for the department and we did as he directed. We recognised his legitimate authority to tell us what to do but we didn't recognise him as our leader. That title fell on the shoulders of one of the area education managers. It was him that people looked to for direction and leadership in times of difficulty. It was him that people wanted in the trenches with them when the going got tough.

Space for your notes

Prompts

- How would you define management and leadership?
- What do you look for in a leader?
- Is your school/college managed or led?

Review of tutorial

'OK. We've looked at the difference between management and leadership and asked if there is in fact any difference. Now we need to look at the differences between education leadership and leadership as exercised in other sectors or industries. 'Do you think there is any difference?' Martin asked.

'I don't know if it's a difference, but I do think it is really important that any manager or leader understands the function that they are managing.'

'Why?'

'Credibility. In the table you just gave me, one of the functions of the leader was to be the leading professional. People want to be led by someone who understands the problems and issues they face. So police officers want to be led by someone who knows what it's like to walk the beat, and nurses want to be led by clinicians, not business graduates who know the cost of everything but have no idea of the value of holding a person's hand as they die.'

'You sound passionate about this.'

'I am. I've had idiots imposed on me who were the friends of senior managers but had no clue about the business. People trust those that understand the needs of the job. You can't fool staff. If a manager doesn't understand the job, their staff will run rings around them.'

'Let's leave that for the moment. I do think that education leadership is different from leadership in other sectors. For example, Handy and Aitkin argue that it's relatively easy to run a private company because even if it has more than one objective all decisions can be reduced to monetary terms and the one that maximises future cash flow selected. Which makes decision making much easier.'

'That's a simplistic view which would be contested by most people who work in the private sector,' I said. 'They will point to the difficulties faced by modern companies in satisfying the often competing demands of stakeholders, such as care for the environment, union demands, social responsibilities and so on. If you don't believe me just ask BP about the oil spill in the Gulf of Mexico.'

'But the aim remains to maximise profits, doesn't it? said Martin.

'No. That's also a fallacy. To maximise profits, you have to accept an increased level of risk. Companies are run by directors who are employed by shareholders. Every shareholder wants a return on their investment but they don't want directors to take unreasonable risk. Directors know this so they aim to achieve satisfactory returns which will satisfy the investors without risking the company's future,' I said.

'I'll bow to your greater understanding of company finance, but would you accept that making a profit is the most important objective of any business?'

'To remain profitable and in business, yes.'

'OK then. Here's the important point: education doesn't have a generally accepted set of objectives, let alone one that is considered paramount. Questions relating to the aims of education are inextricably linked with people's values, their views about the nature of the person and the "good life", and the role education has in preparing people to play a full role in the political process and society generally.'

'So how does that affect the education leader?'

'Because, as Winch argues, if the aims are contested it is difficult for the leader to establish a vision or set of aims that all the stakeholders can agree on. You can see how difficult it is when typically the aims of education have been listed as: to provide an appropriate education, whatever that means, contribute to the spiritual, moral and physical development of the student, provide certification of learning, develop the student's social skills, to enable students to exercise their rights and responsibilities as future citizens, prepare students for the world of work and meet the government's economic agenda.'

'I don't think I'd like to be the one who has to square that particular circle.'

'It gets worse. Many writers argue that, because education is concerned with providing access to knowledge, encouraging enquiry and the inculcation of truth, it has a moral purpose. Hodgkinson argues that any leader in education must be aware of these purposes and suggests that, if education is special, then educational leadership must also be special or different.'

'I think what you've just said supports my earlier argument that education leaders need to be experienced educationalists,' I said. 'Because, in order to make good decisions or sell their vision, the education leader must take these competing views into account before arriving at a decision or course of action.'

'I didn't say I disagreed with your argument, only that we would come back to it. Despite claims that education is special, we know that the use of commercial practices and management tools is rife in education. As these become the norm, there is a risk that education leaders will become more like commercial managers and forget their heritage.'

'So you agree with Ball that the use of performative practices by education leaders changes what they do and how they see themselves?' I said (see Tutorial 1).

'To some extent. But, as Gleeson and Shain argued, the idea that principals have gone over to the "dark side" of managerialism is overstated. I think most principals still try to accommodate the changes required by managerialism while recognising that they can't manage a school or college in the same way you would a factory. Of course what happens when the current generation of leaders retires is another question.'

'Or when the free schools movement gathers real momentum?'

'Maybe, but that is a whole new can of worms which I would like to leave for the time being. If you want to see what I think about it, have a look at my website www.pearsoned.com/mcgrathandcoles. In the meantime I want to finish by looking at power because without some form of power leaders can't function.'

'OK.'

'Giddens suggests that power can be described as the ability of individuals or groups to get their own way even when others disagree with or resist their objectives. However, Johnson and Scholes (1998:127) see power as the extent to which individuals or groups are able to persuade or coerce people into following their directions.'

'Both definitions seem to fit nicely with Northouse's definition of leadership, where leaders influence the actions of followers,' I said.

'I agree. But you need to think about where a leader's power comes from. Now, there are various models of power, but the one I like best is based upon the work of French and Raven from the 1960s. They identified five power sources that a person, real or corporate, could exercise to encourage or compel compliance. These are: first, reward – where a person has the capacity to grant or withhold rewards; second, coercion – where a person has the capacity to impose sanctions or punishments on another; third, legitimacy – where the person's position is deemed to carry with it the right to command compliance or action; fourth, expertise – where an individual's expertise in a particular area is deemed sufficient to command either action or compliance and, finally, referent or charismatic leadership – which results from the person's actions and personality.'

'Which is the best one to have?' I asked.

'Of the five sources, French and Raven believe that referent power is the most powerful and widest ranging as it is able to influence people over time and distance. They also point out that anyone who can exercise more than one type of power achieves synergy, meaning that when joined together two or more types of power provide a greater level of power than the sum of the individual parts.'

'It seems a bit old; surely someone has come up with a better model in the past 50 years.'

'You'd think so, but French and Raven's is a seminal article and is still widely referred to today. Handy tried to update French and Raven's list. Here, this table compares the two. As you can see, Handy's ideas correspond closely with French and Raven's.' Martin gave me a second handout (see page 63).

'Basically Handy has reworded French and Raven's list.'

'But he's also added a sixth source of power – negative power,' I said.

'Yes. Handy describes negative power as the ability to delay, disrupt or stop things happening. He makes the point that the level of negative power a person can exercise is not related to the position they hold. So a person quite low down the school hierarchy can disrupt things if they are not happy.'

'I've seen how that operates. I was working in one school when a new principal took over and she made the mistake of not inviting the caretaker to attend the first school meeting. It was January and mysteriously the heating in her office and the staffroom went on the blink for a week.'

'That's a good example of negative power. Of course, in a culture of managerialism the importance of administration has increased, and this provides opportunities for senior administrators to exercise negative power in terms of agenda setting, blocking changes and deciding how new initiatives should be implemented and operated. Indeed, Rosenfield and Wilson suggest that those who have the power to set the agenda for meetings and other discussions have the potential to wield significant negative power.'

'The same principal I was talking about always insisted on writing the minutes for any meeting she attended. This allowed her to have the final say on what was decided at any meeting she chaired.'

'It's always useful to have control of the minutes, because they are the official record of what has been decided. Everything else in a meeting is just talk. She sounds like an interesting character,' Martin said.

'She was quite a powerful principal but not very well liked. I was never able to work out if her ability to exercise power was linked to her position or some mixture of position, personal traits and abilities,' I replied.

'With most principals it will be a mixture. Staff accept that the principal derives legitimate authority from their position and therefore they have the power to give rewards or exercise coercion, even if that is restricted to a pat on the back or a telling-off. So, immediately they have at their disposal three sources of power. If they are also respected as a teacher and educationalist, then they can exercise expert power. That just leaves personal or charismatic power.'

'Which of course some people have and others don't,' I said.

'True. But if a principal is charismatic or has a powerful personality they will, potentially, be able to exercise enormous power over their staff. But remember that while a leader's charisma/personality can inspire some people it can put others off. You only need to look at people's opinions of Tony Blair when he was first elected.'

"Some people saw charm and openness and others saw just another snake-oil salesman,' I said.

'Exactly. Now I'll leave you with one final thought: Middlehurst suggests that power is a resource that leaders can use but that leadership is the medium or channel through which power is exercised. On that profound note we'll end for today. Next time we're looking at trait theory, so see what you can find on it and emotional intelligence (EI).'

Nat's reflection

09 October

Like most people who have never worked in the private sector, Martin thinks that the only objective of private enterprise is to maximise profits. It's a lot more complicated than that. However, I do agree with him that it's not as complicated as education.

I couldn't believe that we have no agreed set of aims for education so I did a Google search. It appears that it was only in 1999 that the English education system tried to formulate a set of education aims. Not surprisingly, these were based on the previous implicit aims which were, according to Winch and Gingell (2004: 8), 'To provide a basic mass education for the future working population, one that would combine basic literacy and numeracy with supportive attitude to the existing social and political order'. Straight away I can see that a lot of people would disagree with such a narrow set of aims. For a start, it says nothing specific about spiritual, moral or physical development.

In Tutorials 1 and 2 Martin and I discussed how managerialism, performativity and organisational culture constrained the educational leaders' freedom of action. People's different conception of the aims of education is another set of constraints that I'll have to juggle with when I become a principal. Without any agreement on the aims of education, it's going to be hard to agree a vision for the organisation.

I think I'll do a bit more work on the sources of power. It's interesting that the role of principal carries with it at least three sources of power: reward – they can promote people; coercion – they can impose sanctions on people, and legitimacy – generally everyone recognises that they are in charge. I can think of several people who exercised considerable power and got a lot of things done just by using those three levers. So if I can add expert power and even a modicum of personal power to the mix, potentially I could exercise enormous power – even as a deputy. Mind you, the boss might not be too happy. She could see me as a threat. Probably the best thing to do is practise exercising my power discreetly until I become the boss.

Space for your notes

Prompts

- Do you think that education leadership is different? If so how is it different from leading medical staff in a hospital or social workers in a local authority?
- What sources of power does your current principal rely on?

Record of tutorial

Summary notes from tutorial held on 6 October

- Management is concerned with setting objectives, organising resources, motivating staff, measuring and monitoring results and developing people.
- Leadership is a process in which an individual influences a group of individuals to achieve a common goal.
- Many commentators argue that it is pointless to try to differentiate between management and leadership, as time, place and context can determine if an act is one of administration, management or leadership.
- Until about 1979, 'administration' was the preferred term used to describe what principals did. Between 1980 and about 1994, 'management' replaced 'administration' as the preferred term before it in turn was replaced by 'leadership'.
- However, while the name given to what principals do has changed over the years, their duties have not changed significantly: that is, they have always been involved with winning the hearts and minds of people in order to meet the changing needs of pupils/students/staff/parents/local and central government.

- It's very difficult to define 'leadership' but like such terms as 'beauty' and 'love' we can recognise it when we see it.

- Instead of trying to define management and leadership, it may be more useful to try to identify what managers and leaders do.

- In summary, it may be that the difference between management and leadership is a state of mind. Management is concerned with the here and now and many of its functions have their basis in science: for example, the use of figures for accounting and statistical purposes. Leadership is concerned with the future and the dreams of both the leader and her followers. Leadership is concerned with feelings and is an art.

- The title of leader can never be claimed by someone. It has to be bestowed on the person by her followers.

- Leadership in the commercial sector is about satisfying the demands of various stakeholders such as the public, customers, staff and shareholders. To achieve this it is necessary to maintain an acceptable level of profits while ensuring the continued existence of the organisation.

- The aims of education are more diffuse and contested. This is because they are tied up with people's values and beliefs.

- The aims of education include: the spiritual, moral and physical development of the person; preparing students to play a full part in the social, economic and political life of society; the certification of learning, and meeting the government's economic agenda.

- To be successful, the education leader needs to be aware of these competing aims and have a philosophy that enables him/her to navigate a course of action that both recognises and deals with these demands.

- To deal with the competing demands, the education leader requires a deep understanding of the different aims of education otherwise they, and the course of action they propose, will lack credibility.

- The title of principal does not necessarily mean that the holder will be recognised as a leader. Only followers can bestow the title of leader. However, that does not mean that a principal can't influence a group of people to achieve an objective that they have set. They can achieve such objectives by the exercise of power.

- Johnson and Scholes define power as the extent to which an individual or group is able to persuade or coerce others into following a course of action.

- French and Raven identified five sources of social power. These were reward, coercion, legitimacy, expertise and personal or charismatic power.
- The first three sources of power will be held by most/all principals. Many will also be experts in their chosen sector of education. However, the exercise of power does not mean that the person is a leader.
- True leaders tap into the fifth source of power and exercise personal/charismatic power. It is the power of 'personality' that creates a personal relationship between the leader and the led.
- The exercise of such personal power extends beyond the confines of work and can inspire people to achieve beyond what is expected of them.
- The sources of power are additive, meaning that a synergy is created when someone is able to exercise more than one type of power.
- Handy amended the terms used to describe the sources of power and added a sixth source – negative power.
- Negative power can be exercised by anyone in the organisation and there is no correlation between the impact that it may have and the position in the hierarchy of the person exercising the power. Thus, an administrator might use bureaucratic procedures to block or delay the implementation of a policy.

Implications of learning for my leadership style

I have widespread experience of education, therefore I do have credibility with staff. However, very often I think of what I do in management terms. I don't use it as an opportunity to exercise leadership. I issue instructions (nicely) and I monitor actions taken and results achieved, but I don't seek to inspire people. I don't show them the value of their actions or the impact they have on learners. I need to use each meeting I have with staff as an opportunity to show them how their actions contribute to the achievement of the organisation's vision. Every member of staff needs to feel that they have a vital part to play in achieving our objectives and that these objectives are educationally worthwhile.

Somewhere, I read or did I hear it in a film? Help, my memory's going – we don't love people for what they are but for how they make us feel about ourselves. That's what I need to do. I have to make people feel good about themselves and help them to believe that what they do is worthwhile. If I can do that, they will see me as someone who motivates and inspires them – a leader.

Figure 3.1 The interrelationship between management, administration, leadership and power

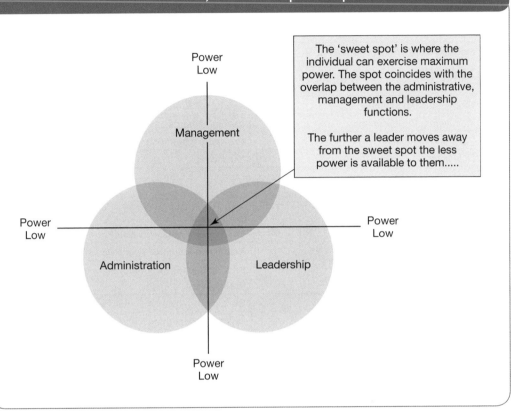

Power
Low

Management

The 'sweet spot' is where the individual can exercise maximum power. The spot coincides with the overlap between the administrative, management and leadership functions.

The further a leader moves away from the sweet spot the less power is available to them.....

Power
Low

Power
Low

Administration

Leadership

Power
Low

Handout

Table 3.1 The differing perspectives of managers and leaders

Managers are concerned with …	Leaders are concerned with …
The present	The future
Plans	Vision
Maintenance of systems	The big picture
Maintaining the status quo	Leading change
Providing feedback	Providing inspiration
Objectives	Outcomes

Table 3.2 The activities undertaken by managers and leaders

Managers are concerned with …	Leaders are concerned with …
Monitoring and control	Exercising influence over followers
Providing a sense of order	Providing a sense of purpose and direction for followers
Spreading organisational culture	Building organisational culture
Doing things right	Doing the right things
Acting in accordance with managerial requirements	Acting as the leading professional internally and the chief executive externally
Dealing with complexity within and around the organisation	Dealing with change and the effects of change
Producing order and consistency	Producing change and movement
Planning and budgeting	Vision building and strategising
Organisational structure and staffing	Aligning people behind common objectives
Problem solving	Problem seeking
Economy and efficiency	Effectiveness
Staying on the right path	Making new paths

(Tables 3.1 and 3.2 are adapted from the work of Fidler, 1997; Grace, 1995; Handy, 1992; Law and Glover, 2000; Middlehurst, 1993; Northouse, 2007)

Table 3.3 Sources of power

French and Raven	Handy
Ability to reward	Ability to provide resources or rewards to staff
Coercion – the ability to force staff to obey instructions	Physical – ability to force staff to obey instructions
Legitimacy – power that comes with, say, the office of principal	Positional – power that comes with, say, the office of principal
Expertise	Expertise
Charismatic/referent power – a personality trait that draws people to another person even if they don't know them personally	Personal power – a personality trait that draws people to another person even if they don't know them personally
	Negative power – the ability to cause disruption

(Adapted from French and Raven, 1960; Handy, 1993; Rosenfield and Wilson, 1999)

Additional information on the issues covered by this tutorial can be found at/in:

- www.pearsoned.com/mcgrathandcoles
- **French, J. and Raven, B.H.** (1960) *The basis of social power*, in Cartwright, D. (ed.) *Studies of Social Power*. Ann Arbour: Institute for Social Research.
- **Northouse, P.G.** (2007) *Leadership Theory and Practice*, (4th edn). London: Sage. Ch.1.
- **Winch. C. and Gingell, J.** (2004) *Philosophy and Educational Policy: A Critical Introduction*. London: Routledge Falmer.

Trait and emotional intelligence theory

Aim of tutorial

By the end of the tutorial you will be able to list a set of traits that are commonly associated with leadership, explain why trait theory is still important and how it relates to the newer theory of emotional intelligence.

Contents

- Background to and definition of trait theory
- Strengths and limitations of trait theory
- Why trait theory is still popular?
- How to use your knowledge of trait theory to your advantage
- Emotional intelligence theory described and defined
- Is emotional intelligence just another name for trait theory?
- Can emotional intelligence be learnt?
- Is emotional intelligence an essential attribute for all managers and leaders?
- How to apply emotional intelligence theory in your organisation

Nat's reflection

13 October

Today, we start our discussion of actual leadership theories. I feel on firmer ground here as most of the management and leadership courses that I've been on dealt with this or that leadership theory. But what I never liked was the idea that all I had to do to become a good leader was follow the trainer's recipe and hey, presto, I'd be transformed Cinderella-like from a down-trodden and unremarkable manager to the belle of the leadership ball.

No, it takes more to become a leader than just applying a theory. I think leadership is a bit like following a recipe for stew! First, you throw into the pot all the leadership theories you have, followed by your experiences of management and leadership both good and bad and finally your own personality. You then give it one almighty stir and let it simmer in the pressure cooker of everyday work. What comes out is your own unique leadership style.

Time to go.

Review of tutorial

Martin was watching a scene from *The American President* when I entered. Looking up, he waved me to a seat. '**I've offered to do the Saturday morning wind-up slot at a conference next week. I want something interesting but light. I thought I might use some film scenes as examples of the importance of integrity in leadership.**'

'Well you've got a good one there,' I said.

'**True enough. But we need to crack on. Today, I want to look at trait theory and emotional intelligence or EI as it's called. I take it you've done a bit of reading?**'

'Yes,' I nodded.

'OK. So what can you tell me about trait theory?'

'It is based on the **great man theory** of leadership which I suppose goes all the way back to the start of civilisation. This was the idea that great statesmen and military leaders had certain innate characteristics that made them special and which enabled them to be great leaders. So a lot of time was spent searching for and describing these attributes.'

'The ancients actually went further than just describing these characteristics. The ruling classes tried to instil them in their children. Take the Romans, for example. Julius Caesar was trained from a very early age to be both a military and political leader. He was taught military and political history along with philosophy and rhetoric by Greek teachers. And most importantly he was expected to demonstrate appropriate behaviour in all he did – even as a child.'

'Didn't the English do something similar in the nineteenth century with public schools?'

'I think that is a reasonable analogy. If from an early age you tell a child that he, and it was always a he, was born to lead, most will believe you and see leadership as their right. This gives them the essential self-confidence to be a leader. Without which, they will never make it. So how did the great man theory become trait theory?'

'I'm not entirely sure when one morphed into the other, but I suspect it happened at the start of the twentieth century when people started to write about management,' I said.

'Indeed it did. Up until the mid-1840s most organisations were owned either by a single person, family or partnership. But as the industrial revolution gathered pace and business enterprises expanded, more capital was required so the idea of establishing companies became popular. The first Companies Act was passed in 1844, but limiting the liability of shareholders to the value of their shares was not introduced until 1855, and after that a whole raft of Companies Acts followed in 1862, 1908, 1929 and 1948. Since then, various consolidation acts have been passed, the most significant in 1985–6 and 1989.'

'And how is this relevant to trait theory?' I asked.

'Sorry, I'm just showing off. Prior to the growth of companies, most businesses were run by the owner or partners on a daily basis. But it was impossible for the shareholders who owned the new businesses to do the same so they appointed managers and directors.'

'And, naturally, the people appointed were selected on the basis of the charac-teristics that they displayed and shared with other leaders and managers of the time,' I said.

'That's exactly the point that Richmon and Allison make when they say that trait theory is concerned with the identification and analysis of the qualities of leaders. Unfortunately, the theory only concentrates on one aspect of leader-ship, that is, the traits of the leader, and ignores context and style. Even so, it continues to exercise considerable influence on how people see leadership. Even the most cursory review of adverts for principals shows how pervasive the theory is, with long lists of essential and desirable traits being specified. But what do you think is its greatest weakness?'

'I think it is probably impossible to provide a definitive list of traits that distin-guish leaders from non-leaders.'

'Exactly, but that hasn't stopped writers from compiling numerous lists. Here, this handout gives you an indication of the diverse traits that have been con-sidered important over the years (see page 81, Table 4.1). As you can see, I've tried to show where writers have used the same or similar words to describe a trait by lining them up across all four headings. But even so, there is more disparity than agreement.'

I studied the table for a few moments before saying, 'Actually I'm surprised at the amount of agreement between the lists. I've seen some which are signifi-cantly different.'

'That's probably because they have been based on the requirements of a specific sector or industry. For example, it's fairly common to see physical courage included in military lists and you would be surprised how many men-tion a sense of humour.'

'What's Handy's helicopter effect?' I asked.

'It's the ability of the leader to rise above the specifics of a situation and instead see them as just one component of the broader environment in which the organisation is operating. So, instead of seeing one field, the leader can see the entire farm. Interestingly, he also suggested that leaders appeared to enjoy good health and came from the upper socio-economic level of society.'

'But there are plenty of leaders who didn't enjoy good health. President Roosevelt won four elections yet he suffered with ill health. And President Lincoln didn't come from the upper levels of society. There are numerous others that don't fit the descriptions provided,' I said.

'Which is another weakness of the theory – as soon as you posit a list of desirable characteristics, someone can point to an exception. That said, I do think that self-confidence is essential, as is a certain level of intelligence. But not too much intelligence. It's no good having a highly intelligent leader if her intelligence makes it difficult for the followers to understand her. That's why many highly intelligent leaders play down their intelligence. They want to present themselves as just regular folk – President Clinton, who was one of the most intellectually gifted presidents of all time, used this tactic.'

'I was reading in *The Times* that President Obama suffers from a similar problem. Even his staff find him distant and remote – too much like the law professor he once was.'

'Which is not something that any leader can appear to be. What other disadvantages can you think of?'

'Trait theory concentrates solely on the personality of the leader and ignores the needs of the followers and the situation in which leadership is exercised. But I think the fundamental weakness has to be that as traits are inherent in the individual they can't be learnt. Which means that they can't be taught or developed to any great extent. Yet there are many stories that contradict this. For example, Warren Buffet, the second richest man in the world, is renowned for the relationship he has built up with his staff, colleagues and shareholders and the power of his communication skills. Yet, as a young man, he was shy and lacked social skills. A weakness he identified and set about correcting through training and practice.'

'Very good. But what about strengths: does trait theory have any?'

'Well, it's been around for a very long time and is well established in people's minds.' I said.

'True, it's probably the most researched leadership theory we have.'

'It's simple. Everyone can understand it and it "feels right". People want to believe that their leaders are different or special. That they possess special characteristics, which the average person does not have or at least does not have to the same level, such as sociability, charm, intelligence, courage, persistence or whatever.'

'And therein lies the problem. Followers want to put their leader on a pedestal and, as we all know, leaders are only human…'

'So it's just a matter of time before they fail to live up to our expectations and we pull them down' I said.

'Precisely. But the emphasis on what qualities a leader should have is useful because it does provide us with an idea of what to look for in a leader. Employers can use it as a first sieve when attempting to identify potential leaders. And want-to-be leaders can use it to identify aspects of their personality that they need to work on if they want to be considered a leader. If you have a look at Table 4.2 (see handout page 82), I've given some examples of the traits that you might see listed as essential in an advert for teacher or manager and tried to show how you can demonstrate that you have these traits in an interview.'

I quickly scanned the table and then looking up said, 'Sneaky. I like it.'

Nat's reflection

15 October

OK, what do I reckon are the six most important traits that a leader needs to have?

- Self-confidence — no one will follow a person who appears unsure or dithers. Just ask Gordon Brown. Now the important word here is 'appears'. I might have my doubts and fears but I can't afford to show them to 'my followers'. When I first became a teacher I was very nervous about standing in front of the class but my mentor told me I should never show fear. So I acted as if I was confident and sure. And pretty quickly my confidence grew and became real. So it's possible to 'fake it until you make it'.

- Intelligence — I'm working in education so intellect and professional knowledge are respected. I need to demonstrate through my actions that I know what I'm talking about. So I need to be honest with staff when they ask a question. If I don't have the answer, I need to avoid bluffing and say something like 'I don't know the answer to that but I know a woman that does' and 'I'll get back to you'. Then I must keep my promise and get back to them.

- Helicopter effect – someone in the organisation has to rise above the day-to-day hustle and bustle and be able to view the organisation in its totality and not as a series of disparate units. As leader, I have to be able to do that and to encourage others in the organisation to do the same.

- Persistence – I need to keep going even when the going gets tough. I can't give up at the first obstacle or setback I meet. Once I've established my vision or plan of action, I have to pursue it relentlessly. But I also need to remember that one definition of madness is to keep doing the same thing but expect different results. Therefore, I need to be flexible enough to change my tactics while still working towards my objectives.

- Integrity – people follow those they respect and trust. So I need to demonstrate integrity in my dealings with staff.

- Responsibility – I have to be willing to take responsibility for the organisation's failings when things go wrong and not just blame the staff. But the staff have to also take responsibility for their actions and decisions.

Hang on. Where's motivation gone? I need a seventh trait. (Just shows the problem with trait theory!) I need to be able to motivate myself and the staff. One way is to be a role model and demonstrate that I am willing to work hard and muck in and help staff when it's required.

It's just occurred to me that the seven traits I've listed are just a reflection of what I look for in a leader or are traits that I think I already possess. In other words, I could be conning myself about how important they are to other people/followers. Maybe I should do a bit of research with my staff and find out what they think.

Space for your notes

Prompts

● List the six traits that you believe leaders require.

● To what extent do you think traits can be developed or taught?

● What leadership traits do you have?

Review of tutorial

'What about emotional intelligence and leadership? I've been doing a bit of reading on how EI relates to leadership but I have to say it doesn't seem that different from trait theory,' I said.

'It certainly has some similarities, but one of the major claims made for it is that unlike traits it is possible to develop peoples' emotional intelligence.'

'I can think of a couple of managers I've endured who had zero emotional intelligence. I can't see how they could be developed.'

'Goleman wrote a couple of really good articles for the *Harvard Business Review*. If you want a good overview of his ideas you need to read both. Basically, he says that if a person wants to become emotionally intelligent they have to be willing to change and to work at it over a significant period to achieve that change. He argues that it's a complete waste of time sending a person on a two-day training course and expect them to change. What's required is a long-term development programme that uses teaching methods associated with the affective domain.'

'You mean discussion, reflection, role-play and feedback?'

'Yes. He suggests you need a coach or mentor who can monitor your actions and provide feedback on how you are doing. So your mentor will observe you at work, sit in on meetings and see how you deal with staff and colleagues and then discuss your actions with you.'

'It sounds like you could also do a bit of **360-degree appraisal** and ask your line manager, colleagues and other staff how you were performing.'

'You could, if you were that brave and they were willing to be honest and frank in their feedback. But tell me, what do you know about the actual theory?'

'Not a lot,' I said honestly.

'OK. Goleman says that emotional intelligence comprises five interlinked concepts. They are: self-awareness, self-regulation, motivation, empathy and social skills. Let's take them one at a time. Self-awareness is the ability to evaluate your own strengths and weaknesses without false modesty or arrogance and to share this information with others when required. It's also about understanding how your emotions, both negative and positive, impact on your mood and actions.'

'So it's about knowing yourself,' I said.

'Yes. "Self-awareness" is not a term that appears in many trait lists but it has similarities with "self-confidence". Genuine self-confidence comes from knowing your strengths and weaknesses and not being afraid of saying that you're good at this but poor at that. It's also usually accompanied by a good dose of self-deprecating humour.

'So what's self-regulation about?'

'That's about being able to control and deal with your emotions. Not to let them rule you. To think before you act. That's something we all need to improve. Too often we get angry and say something, usually to the wrong person at the wrong time and without knowing all the facts.'

'That's definitely a fault of mine. I seem to be able to put up with a load of grief for ages and then blow my top over the smallest problem, usually at the most inopportune moment,' I said.

'Self-regulation requires us to reflect before we act. If you can stay calm under pressure, people will see you as measured in your judgements. They won't be afraid to tell you bad news because they know that you won't erupt into anger for no reason. People will consider you trustworthy as someone with patience and consideration. Someone they can trust. What do you think motivation is about?' Martin asked.

'I think it's about a desire to get things done. Which I suppose links with persistence and enthusiasm in trait theory. But I also think it's about passion for the work. This passion can communicate itself to those you work with and in turn motivate them.'

'That's a useful insight. Your passion for the job can motivate others. Their actions then motivate you and before you know it you've built a virtuous circle. But I think you've missed an important element here of what Goleman means by motivation, and that is the ability to remain optimistic and enthusiastic even in the face of failure.'

'In other words, put on a happy face.'

'Smile and the world smiles with you! Don't tell me you're into Hollywood musicals as well as *The West Wing*,' Martin said smiling.

'Guilty as charged,' I said ruefully.

'It's an embarrassing confession to have to make. But as a fan of Broadway musicals I can understand the embarrassment you must feel. It's hard to keep such a "shameful secret", Martin said with mock dark solemnity. 'But it does lead us nicely on to empathy. Empathy is concerned with understanding the emotional make-up of other people and being able to put yourself in their position. It's not the same as sympathy. So you can be empathetic when disciplining a member of staff without feeling sorry for them. I suppose it's about being able to read people's emotional state and respond appropriately.'

'I'm not too bad at that,' I said.

'That's good. If you are empathetic with people, you will find that you can build strong lasting relationships with them.'

'And that helps you to retain your best staff and the support of governors and parents,' I said.

'Yes. Which brings us to social skills. They are about being friendly and approachable. It usually means that you are good at building networks and rapport with groups and individuals, and it's likely that you have a wide range of friends and acquaintances. In works terms, I'd say it's about being friendly with a purpose. Usually that purpose is to exercise influence over your colleagues and staff in some way. So it contains an element of persuasiveness. Leaders need strong social skills to build and maintain teams and to lead change when required. So it's a skill worth developing.'

'I'm not very good at small talk,' I said.

'You don't have to be able to talk to be sociable. The ability to listen is far more important. Everyone wants to talk about themselves but few want to listen. If you can engage with a person and let them be the centre of the conversation, they will enjoy talking and go away thinking that you are great. Staff don't want to hear what you have to say – they've had to listen to you rattle on numerous times. They want to tell you what they think. You don't even have to agree with them; many people are quite happy to go along with a decision, provided they have had the opportunity to express their dissenting views.'

'It's about giving people the opportunity to let off steam.'

'Exactly. Listening is the most powerful thing a leader can do to build trust. But there is one thing I want to stress about these five components, and that is that each element interlinks in some way with the others. For example, remaining optimistic even in bad times demonstrates not only an understanding and control of your emotions but also an understanding of how any negative emotions you show can demotivate staff. By recognising that staff feel afraid, unsure or worried, you are demonstrating empathy and the social skills necessary to navigate through troubled times by finding common ground with followers and building teams.'

'OK. But is there any difference between trait theory and emotional intelligence?' I asked.

'A typical list of traits might include self-confidence, intelligence, initiative, persistence and being able to rise above the day-to-day issues and see the organisation in its entirety – the helicopter effect. Now which of those traits have an emotional element?'

'Self-confidence obviously and probably persistence, but you could have a great deal of emotional intelligence but lack cognitive intelligence and be totally unable to see the big picture.'

'Precisely. I'm certain that a good leader needs emotional intelligence and it may be the most important element of leadership, as Goleman claims, but it's not enough. There are other capacities or traits that the leader needs, such as a certain level of intelligence, and the ability to put task before people when it's required …'

'Should a leader ever put task before people?' I asked, surprised at Martin's claim.

'Robert E. Lee, leader of the Confederate Forces in the American Civil War, said that "To be a good soldier you have to love the army, to be a good general you have to be willing to destroy that which you love". Now that's a fairly dramatic statement but a principal has to put the needs of the school or college above those of the staff. Unpopular measures, which harm individuals, sometimes, have to be taken in the best interests of the organisation.'

'So, is the sole focus on emotional factors the greatest weakness of EI?'

'Some would say so.'

'I'm now wondering whether EI is a separate leadership theory or just a part of trait theory.'

'It is different from trait theory in that it takes into account the feelings and emotions of the followers and requires the leader to react appropriately. You can compare that with trait theory which is entirely focused on the attributes possessed by the leader.'

'So EI focuses on both the leader and her followers.'

'Yes and, to a limited degree, the context in which leadership is exercised.'

'And, of course, events can influence the leader's and followers' emotional state.'

'Exactly. Now EI is a fairly new concept, and as more research is done I'm confident that the basic theory will be developed. In the meantime, it's a valuable addition to the tools that a leader might use because it emphasises the importance of emotion in leadership. Few people realise what a change this has been. As recently as the 1970s and 80s, staff and managers were encouraged to leave their emotions at home and anyone who displayed an emotional response to workplace events was considered suspect.'

'The fabled British stiff upper lip in action,' I said.

'Indeed. Anyway, next time I want to look at style, contingency and situational theory. You have been warned.'

Nat's reflection

17 October

I'm still not sure if EI is a separate theory or not. If I take my list of traits (see page 69) and compare them with Goleman's list of EI factors I get:

Table 4.1 Comparison of common leadership traits with EI factors

Traits	Emotional intelligence	Notes
Self-confidence	Self-awareness	Self-confidence based upon a deep understanding of themselves
Social skills	Social skills	Terms as used are almost synonymous
Motivator	Motivation	The trait descriptor relates to the leader's ability to motivate others. The EI descriptor includes motivation of self and others
Integrity	Self-regulation	If integrity equals dealing honestly and fairly with others, then that is not an emotional trait. However, self-regulation implies an ability to control negative urges that might harm others
Intelligence		No equivalent
Helicopter effect		No equivalent
Responsibility	Self-regulation?	Not sure about this. Does taking responsibility show that you can control and regulate your actions?
	Empathy	No equivalent

OK. There is some overlap between traits and EI factors. But there are also three instances where there is no equivalent term. So that means that EI only accounts for some of the skills required by leaders. Albeit, EI does cover some very important skills.

But what can I learn from EI? Well, I probably talk too much. I need to listen to my staff more. I also need to avoid becoming annoyed. I'm not bad-tempered but very occasionally I do blow my top. That's unprofessional. I need to learn to count to ten, or hundred if need be, before I respond to events.

As for networking, I've never been any good at schmoozing people on the off chance that they might be able to help my career. Maybe that explains my rate of progress up the career ladder! The truth is I'm not willing to invest the time that effective networking requires. What I should do is use the opportunities I get at work to extend my network of contacts. I don't have to build up a social relationship with the people, just a professional one.

Space for your notes

Prompts

- To what extent do you agree that emotional intelligence has five components?
- Do you think that EI is a part of trait theory or a separate theory of leadership? Give reasons for your point of view.

Record of tutorial

Summary notes from tutorial held on 13 October

- Trait theory originated in the nineteenth century and is based on the great man theory.
- The theory seeks to identify the innate traits that a leader requires.
- It is claimed that these traits cannot be learnt.
- Trait theory ignores the context in which leadership is exercised, does not consider the style of leadership exercised or take into account the needs or feelings of the followers. It focuses solely on the leader.
- Trait theory's greatest weakness is that it has proved impossible to provide a definitive list of traits that leaders must have. As soon as a new list is identified, it is possible to point to a recognised leader who did/does not have all the traits specified.
- Trait theory's greatest strengths are that it is very easy to understand, people like to think that their leaders are special in some way and it appeals to people's traditional views of what a leader is: for example, heroic figures like Lincoln.
- Trait theory continues to be widely used as a first sieve to identify potential leadership candidates: for example, see any advert for a new principal or the person spec that accompanies the job application pack.
- Emotional intelligence (EI) is made up of five components:
  - self-awareness – know thyself
  - self-regulation – ability to control your emotions, actions and reactions and not be controlled by them
  - motivation – ability to remain positive, and enthusiastic for the work even when times are bad and to pass this on to followers
  - empathy – ability to understand how people are feeling and respond appropriately
  - social skills – ability to be friendly 'with a purpose' and to listen to people.
- It is claimed that EI can be learnt or developed using teaching methods that are often employed in the affective domain such as discussion, reflection and role-play.
- Training in EI demands commitment over a period of time (6–12 weeks). Old habits have to be unlearnt and replaced with new ways of thinking and acting.

- The question 'Is EI a new leadership theory or just part of trait theory?' is difficult to answer. Trait theory does list characteristics that are covered by emotional intelligence as well as some that aren't. This would imply that EI is just a part of trait theory.

- However, EI takes into account the feeling of followers and requires the leader to respond to these appropriately. EI is also concerned with the context in which leadership is exercised, in that events and environment can affect both the leader's and followers' feeling.

Implications of learning for my leadership style

OK, so what can I take from this session in terms of my leadership style? First, I need to confirm that the seven traits I listed are those that staff and management are looking for. I then need to identify what I can do to demonstrate that I possess these traits. Martin's handout should help me with that. Above all else, I must work on appearing self-confident even when I don't feel confident. I can do that by placing myself in situations that are new and challenging. For me, self-confidence is the basis of leadership: if you don't have faith in yourself, why should anyone else?

In terms of EI, I do need to talk less and listen more to staff and I must avoid my occasional 'blow ups'. It's part of every leader's job to take to task a member of staff that has made a mistake or messed up in some way, but it needs to be done properly and with the minimum of emotion. After all, it's the person's actions that I want to criticise, not the person themselves. So I need to think about my approach.

As for networking I'm never going to be one of those people that goes drinking with the boss and others just because I want to be in their clan. However, I'm far from anti-social. I have very good relationships and networks with colleagues at work. We work well together and there isn't a lot of friction. What I should try to do is extend these good professional relationships beyond my workplace to other schools, colleges and local authorities. In that way, my networks will be based on professional rather than social links. Such links may well help my advancement, but even if they don't I will have people outside the organisation I can call on for help and advice when required.

Figure 4.1 List of traits covered by the five Emotional Intelligence factors

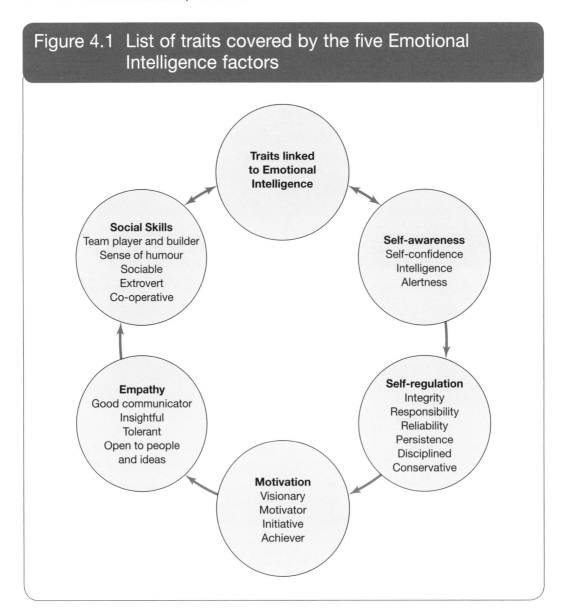

Handout

Traits

Table 4.1 shows four examples of trait lists that have been widely used. While there is some commonality between the lists, there are also some marked differences. The table tries to show the same or similar traits on the same line. However, management writers seldom define what they mean by a word. Readers are therefore compelled to interpret a word in terms of its dictionary definition but this can lead to uncertainty. For example, does Stogdill's use of the word 'insight' imply 'intelligence'?

Table 4.1 Four examples of trait lists

Stogdill 1974	Kirkpatrick and Locke 1991	Handy 1993	TTA 1998
Insight			
	Cognitive ability	Intelligence	Intelligence
Responsibility	Integrity		Reliable/Integrity
Initiative		Initiative	
Persistence	Drive		Persistent/ Commitment
Self-confidence	Self-confidence	Self-confidence	Self-confident
Sociability			Personal impact
Influence	Motivation		Enthusiasm/Energy
Co-operative			
			Adaptable
Concern for achievement of task	Task knowledge		
		Able to see the big picture – Helicopter effect	
Tolerance			

(Adapted from Northouse, 2007; Handy, 1993; TTA, 1998)

Although trait theory is considered outdated and irrelevant by many writers, the reality is that employers still use a form of trait theory when appointing staff (see Table 4.2 overleaf).

Table 4.2 How to demonstrate leadership traits in an interview

Required traits listed in six recent job adverts	How to demonstrate these traits in job applications/interviews
Self-confidence	Be assertive in the interview, maintain eye contact and control your nerves.
Visionary	Give an example of how you envisaged completing a task, then achieved it.
Integrity	Be open and forthright.
Responsible	Demonstrate how you sought out additional responsibilities throughout your career.
Proactive	Give an example of how you anticipated an issue in advance and dealt with it.
Motivator	Don't say (as everyone does) that they motivate by example. Give actual examples of how you have motivated staff and learners.
Team builder	Give an example of how you created a team and allowed the team to operate independently of your control.

Additional information on the issues covered by this tutorial can be found at/in:

- www.pearsoned.com/mcgrathandcoles
- www.businessballs.com
- **Goleman, D.** (1998) What makes a leader *Harvard Business Review*, Nov–Dec 1998. Harvard, Mass: Harvard University.
- **Goleman, D.** (2000) Leadership that gets results. *Harvard Business Review*, March–April 2000. Harvard, Mass: Harvard University.
- **Northouse, P.G.** (2007) *Leadership Theory and Practice*, 4th edn. London: Sage.

Style, contingency and situational theory

Aim of tutorial

By the end of the tutorial you will be able to compare and contrast three popular leadership theories – namely, style, contingency and situational – and identify the strengths and weaknesses of each. You will also continue to identify and develop your own preferred leadership style.

Contents

- Style theory defined and discussed
- Style theory and links to McGregor's X and Y theory of management
- Contingency theory defined and discussed
- Situational theory defined and discussed
- Situational theory – an approach only suitable for middle managers/leaders?
- The need for a leader to utilise several different theories
- The strengths and weaknesses of style, contingency and situational theory

Nat's reflection

20 October

I must be getting old – time seems to be passing faster than it used to! After today I will be half-way through this course. Today we're looking at three more popular leadership theories. Again I know a bit about each so I'm looking forward to an exchange of ideas with Martin.

I have to say that I've enjoyed the chance to exchange my views on management and leadership with Martin. He doesn't know all the answers and he's interested in what I have to say. I've even started to think about what I might do when the sessions end. If I were at an earlier stage in my career, I would probably look at doing an MEd, Ed D or maybe a PhD. But I'm looking to become a principal which means that if I'm successful I won't have the time to sit down, let alone study for a few years. So my options are constrained. At some stage I should have a chat with Martin.

Review of tutorial

Martin's door was open when I arrived but he was nowhere to be seen. I set up the recorder and then perused his bookshelves. There was an eclectic mix including philosophy, politics, education, management, history and leadership, along with the odd book on psychology and sociology. I suppose if you are going to study leadership, you have to dip into these fields as each contains insights into how people think, feel and act, which is what leaders have to understand if they are to be successful.

An out-of-breath Martin entered carrying a bunch of flowers and a large box covered in silver and gold paper and tied with a bow. '**Sorry I'm late, I got stuck in traffic. It's my anniversary today and I dare not go home without a present.**'

'No problem.'

'**OK**,' he said slumping into a chair. '**Today it's style, contingency and situational theory. Let's start with style. Whereas trait theory, and to a lesser extent emotional intelligence theory, is concerned with the personality of the leader, style theory examines the leader's behaviour. The main styles available to a leader are described by Richmon and Allison as "democratic or autocratic, permissive or restrictive and participative or non participative".**'

'I read something about these descriptors. Ohio State University in the late 1940s found that leadership styles clustered around two general types of behaviour: "Initiating Structure", they said, was associated with organising work or the tasks that people perform, while "Consideration Behaviours" were concerned with the relationship between leaders and followers. That's similar to Richmon and Allison's descriptors.'

'**They are, indeed. But what you have to remember about the Ohio studies is that they thought that these behaviours resided at opposite ends of a single continuum. Which means that a leader had to choose between being concerned with the task or relationships with staff. The model implied that they couldn't do both. Here, this sketch will show you what I mean.**' Martin quickly scribbled a simple diagram.

Figure 5.1 Style theory: single continuum model

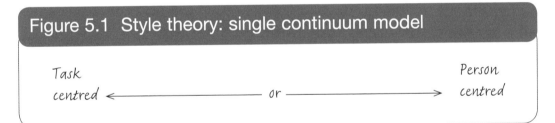

'But we know that good managers can be good at both,' I said.

'**Which is why the model was revised a few years later by staff at the University of Michigan. They renamed the behaviours as Production Orientation and Employee Orientation and argued that the two behaviours should not be thought of as two points on a single continuum but as two discrete continua. This recognised that leaders could be highly task-oriented while still being concerned with the well-being of their staff and staff relations.**' Martin handed me a second sketch.

Figure 5.2 Style theory: two continua

Task-centred descriptors

Autocratic, restrictive,
non-participative, initiating structure,
production orientation

Low _____ High

Person-centred descriptors

Democratic, permissive,
participative, consideration behaviours,
employee orientation

Low _____ High

Looking at the chart I said, 'OK, let me see if I can get this right. Michigan suggests that it's possible for a leader to display any of the following mixes of behaviour. They could be high on task and low on employee orientation or high on task and high on employee orientation or low on task and high on employee orientation or finally low on task and low on employee orientation.'

'Correct. Following the work of Blake and Mouton, it is now generally thought that the most effective leadership style is where the leader is equally concerned with the task and the employee. But I have to say that personally I'm not sure that it is possible for a leader to be highly concerned with both the task and staff all the time. I think it's inevitable that sometimes one or other will dominate.'

'You mean in a crisis or when the importance of getting the job done outweighs concern for people's feelings?'

'Exactly.'

'Personally I can't think of anything worse than a leader who is constantly on steroids,' I said. 'Yes, as leaders we need to maintain a high level of work and good staff relationships but work is made up of peaks and troughs. Sometimes after a really hard or tense time, say an OfSTED inspection, it's right to let the staff freewheel for a bit. You can't keep people working at a high pitch all the time.'

'I agree but that's not what the theorists say.'

'Looking at these diagrams, Style theory seems to share many of the same characteristics as McGregor's X and Y Theory of management,' I said.

'Go on,' said Martin leaning forward.

'Well, McGregor suggested that there were two types of managers. The traditionalists believe that management is a constant battle between lazy workers who are disinterested in work and would do very little if anything unless they weren't constantly monitored, controlled and given directions. He called that approach Theory X. Leaders that focus on task might be Theory X supporters. He used Theory Y to describe the approach taken by managers who believe that people want to work. Such people take an interest and pride in their work and it is the manager's job to provide the right environment for them to develop and grow, which is typical of person-centred leaders.'

'That's an interesting take on McGregor. Often, his theory is used in terms of motivation not leadership but it works nicely. You could develop that idea a bit more.'

Pleased with the pat on the head, I asked: 'Are there any other variations on style theory?'

'Indeed there are. Likert suggested that there were four styles of management, not two. These he described as: the exploitive/authoritarian approach, which is a top-down style and uses threats and punishments to ensure compliance. The benevolent/authoritarian approach, which is similar to the exploitive approach but allows some upward transmission of ideas and communication and gives greater emphasis to rewards than threats. Then there is the consultative style, where goals are set after discussion and team work is encouraged, and finally the participative-group approach. Likert believed that this approach led to commitment to the organisation's goals by all members of staff. To achieve it, it is essential that there are numerous channels of communication both up, down, diagonally and laterally.'

'Is that the same Likert that developed the Likert Scale questions we find in questionnaires?'

'It is. He wrote a lot of good stuff and it's still worth reading. But just in case you think style theory is old and past its sell-by date, Goleman, writing in 2000, also got in on the act when he suggested that there are six leadership

styles that a leader can adopt. A Coercive style involves telling people what to do and demanding immediate compliance. The Authoritative style is less aggressive but still involves saying to people, "Come with me and we can achieve the goals or vision I've set." The Affilliative style is all about creating harmony in the workplace with strong emotional relations between staff and managers where people come first. As you would expect, the Democratic approach involves asking people what they think and seeking consensus. The Pacesetting leader establishes very high standards and offers herself as a role model for staff to imitate. And lastly the leader as a Coach tries to develop people by suggesting that they try this or that approach.'

'Does style theory offer any advice on which approach a leader should adopt in a specific set of circumstances?'

'You have just identified the major weakness of style theory. Identifying the optimum style mix in any given situation remains a key area for further research. About all that can be said is that if things are very bad or very good in an organisation a broadly task-centred approach works well because …'

'If you are doing badly or are in a crisis, you want the leader to be decisive; and if you are doing really well, you are happy to be told what to do because the leader has proved she knows what they are doing,' I said.

'Precisely. Where the organisation is ticking over nicely, a more person-centred approach seems to work best. Broadly speaking, which approach do you think principals use?'

'You'd think that heads would use a more person-centred style than leaders in other sectors, but I have to say that I've come across a number of heads and principals who are very directive and not at all staff-centred,' I said.

'That confirms what Hay McBer found. They compared the leadership style of head teachers with business executives and found that the heads relied on telling people what to do (authoritative) while business executives preferred to use a more strategic approach and set high standards for their staff (pacesetting).'

'Exactly the opposite to what most people would expect,' I said.

'OK, let's move on to contingency theory.'

'Hang on, what about the strengths and weaknesses of style theory?' I asked.

'I have a handout on the strengths and weaknesses of all three theories that we're discussing today. I'll give it to you at the end, and if you have any queries we can discuss them next week. OK?'

'OK.'

Nat's reflection

20 October

What's my style of leadership? Am I interested in the task or the people? Let's see.

I don't like people telling me what to do, especially if they are overbearing and bullying. So I don't bark orders at other people. I also like to avoid conflict. I try to be friendly and non-confrontational. But if people don't do what I ask, I can become aggressive. So what does that make me?

Looking at my career to date, I'd have to say I'm task-driven. I like to get the job done and done well. As a manager, I know that I can't do my job without the support of staff so I try to treat them as I expect to be treated. But if they don't perform, I have a tendency to either take the job off them or do it myself (passive aggression?) or give them a right royal rollicking. Neither approach is the right one. Moderation is required. I have to remember all the assertiveness training that I've undertaken and remain calm, explain where they have gone wrong and insist that they do it again. My criticisms have to be directed at what they did and not at them personally.

The trouble is that we all tend to resort to type under pressure. Basically I have a Type A personality. I'm competitive and can become aggressive if people mess me about. As was clear from last week's session on emotional intelligence, I must become the master of my emotions and learn to use them to my advantage, rather than let them dictate my response to a situation.

Space for your notes

Prompts

- To what extent are you concerned with getting the job done (task-centred), compared with maintaining good working relationships with staff and colleagues (person-centred)?
- Do you tend to use one approach most of the time or are you comfortable switching between the two (task-centred or person-centred), depending on the situation?
- How assertive are you?

Review of tutorial

'Right, let's have a look at contingency theory now. According to Richmon and Allison, "Contingency theory refers to a theory of formal leadership that uses the interactions of the leader's personality ... and situational favourability ... to predict effective and ineffective leaders". There are several approaches to contingency theory, but the most widely recognised is that developed by Fidler. What do you know about contingency theory?'

'Not a lot. It's not a theory that I've studied or covered in a training course.'

'That's because it's not a very popular theory with trainers. It builds on style theory in so much as the leader's style is still described as either task or relationship motivated. But it goes on to suggest that the leader's effectiveness is contingent upon how well their style fits the context they find themselves in.'

'So what do they mean by context and how do they assess it?'

'It's important to note that the context doesn't relate to the type of organisation you are in: for example, school, college, shop or factory. It relates to the circumstances in which leadership is exercised and it's assessed using three factors: namely, the relationship between the leader and followers. Is it good or bad? The level of structure that exists in the task which followers are engaged in: for example, staff in McDonald's perform highly structured tasks with written guidance on how to perform every task, while teachers have very little structure to the work they do. Even with managerialism and OfSTED, teachers still enjoy a great deal of discretion in how they perform their job. And, finally, the positional power: which is, to what extent does the leader have the power to reward or punish followers? Obviously principals have significant but not unlimited power in this area.'

'And it's a combination of these three factors that determines the favourableness of the situation?'

'Yes. Do you fancy trying to work out all the permutations?' Martin asked with a malicious grin.

'I'm always up for a challenge. Give me a piece of paper,' I said and spent the next few minutes drafting out the various combinations. Finally I handed Martin my list.

Table 5.1 List of possible combinations

Relationship	Structure	Personal power
Good	High	High
Good	High	Low
Good	Low	High
Good	Low	Low
Poor	High	High
Poor	High	Low
Poor	Low	High
Poor	Low	Low

Martin looked at the list and smiled. 'So which is the best and worst position for the leader to be in?'

'Well, clearly the best position is the first where the leader has good relations with staff, the task is highly structured and they have a lot of personal/positional power. While the worst is where relations are poor, the structure is low and the leader's personal power is also low.'

'Correct. But what is not so clear in contingency theory is what the leader should do when the situation is not entirely favourable to them.'

'You would think that they should change their style of leadership to suit the context.'

'But therein lies the problem. Contingency is basically a personality theory. It assumes that the leader's personality is fixed and difficult to change. Therefore, if anything has to change it's the context. But it doesn't give any guidance on how this can be done.'

'That seems daft. It's usually very difficult to change the nature of work performed and it's not easy to increase the level of personal power that you have. Besides, you do have to ask why a load of people should be messed about just because the leader doesn't fit in.'

'I agree. But the theory hopes to avoid such problems by being predictive. In other words, it has been suggested that organisations can develop leadership profiles of staff and from these identify which situations a particular person is most likely to be successful in based on past performance. The idea is that some leaders will fare better than others in situations where the conditions are less than entirely favourable. Management can then select the most appropriate candidate for each post. So the theory is very realistic in the sense that it doesn't expect leaders to be successful in all situations.'

'But if there is a mistake made, you still end up with a square peg in a round hole.

'Yes.'

'And if you are appointing someone from outside your organisation, you don't have their "leadership profile" to assist you.'

'You're pre-empting some of the points made on the handout about strengths and weaknesses (see page 105). Anyway, before we finish with contingency theory, have you ever heard of John Adair?'

'You mean his idea that leadership is concerned with ensuring that the task is completed while the needs of the group and individuals are met?'

'That's the one. His approach has been called "functional" or "action-centred leadership". He argues that leadership is more about doing the right things and acting correctly than personality or being in the right place at the right time. His theory suggests that leadership involves balancing the needs of the task, the group and individuals. He uses three interlocking circles to explain his ideas like this,' Martin said and showed me a diagram of Adair's leadership model.

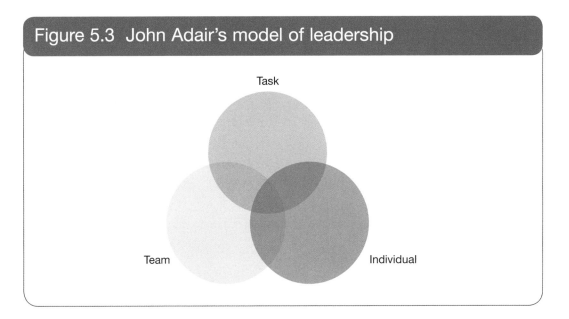

Figure 5.3 John Adair's model of leadership

I looked at the graphic and waited for Martin to continue. **'Can you see,'** he said, **'that his ideas are very similar to those of modern contingency theorists who are concerned with task, people and situation? But he departs from the orthodox theory by suggesting that, if there is a mismatch between the context and the leader, it is the leader's duty to adjust their behaviour. Which is very much in line with what you said.'**

Nat's reflection

21 October

Martin seems to be dealing with the leadership theories in chronological order. First came trait theory, from the start of the twentieth century, which is concerned with the innate characteristics of the leader. Style theory started in the 1940s and moved on from looking at what the leader was to what they did; and now contingency theory, from the 1960s, which combines style theory with consideration of the context in which leadership is exercised.

But what does contingency theory mean for me? I suppose it reminds me of the need to analyse the situation I find myself in. Currently, I have good relationships with most of the staff, but teaching is an unstructured job so I'm not in a position to tell them how to do their job, especially in the classroom. However, because the principal supports me, I can exercise a degree of personal power over them. Unfortunately, my power is limited because, while I can make their professional lives difficult, I'm not in a position to promote a member of staff or award a pay increase. So my contingency profile would be:

● Relationship – High
● Structural – Low/medium
● Personal power – Medium.

So what does that mean? I suppose, because I have a good relationship with most staff and sound professional skills, I am able to exercise some influence over how staff work in the classroom. And most of them know that I have the ear of the head so they probably treat me as if I have more power than I actually do. So I'm in a reasonable position to exercise leadership. Of course if I were to become principal, the profile would become high – medium – high, which explains the difference between the principal and a mere member of the SMT.

Is there anything I can do to change the profile? I know I'm supposed to change the context and not myself but that's impractical in my situation, so I think I should try to exercise greater influence over what goes on in the classroom by improving my own professional standing in the school. Perhaps I need to make more explicit my philosophy of teaching and see if I can motivate the staff with my ideas.

Space for your notes

Prompts

- Using the three descriptors – relationship, structure and personal power – analyse the favourableness of the situation for your principal and yourself (if you hold a managerial position).
- Consider what strategies you might adopt to improve your standing against all three descriptors.

Review of tutorial

'OK, so that leaves us with situational theory. According to Richmon and Allison, "It examines the interaction between situational variables and the leader's behaviour". What do you know about it?' Martin asked.

'I went on a middle managers' training course years ago. You know the type that tells you this is how you manage staff, and the model they used was situational leadership. They gave us a book by Kenneth Blanchard called the "One

Minute Manager". The theory focuses on leadership within given situations, and basically it argues that different situations require different types of leadership, and that therefore the leader has to adapt her style to fit the situation.'

'Go on.'

'Well, it suggests that the leader needs to use a mixture of directive and supportive behaviour when dealing with staff. Directive behaviour involves giving staff extensive, detailed and unambiguous instructions on how to complete a task. By contrast, supportive behaviour is about building up the person's self-confidence by telling them that you have faith in their ability to do the job and being there for them if they run into difficulties.'

'Correct. Can you see that this theory clearly owes its origins to style theory? It's concerned with both task and people. But it also owes something to contingency theory because it tries to take on board the context in which the leader acts.'

I nodded in agreement and Martin continued, **'So what are the permutations that these two factors can create?'**

'Well, it's easier to write them down. Where's my piece of paper gone?' I asked, and finding it started to draw the situational grid.

Table 5.2 The situational grid (51–54)
The four leadership styles

(S3) Supporting	(S2) Coaching
• *High supportive behaviour*	• *High directive behaviour*
• *Low directive behaviour*	• *High supportive behaviour*
(S4) Delegating	(S1) Directing
• *Low supportive behaviour*	• *High directive behaviour*
• *Low directive behaviour*	• *Low supportive behaviour*

I handed the drawing to Martin and after looking at it he said, **'OK, tell me what each style means.'**

I took a deep breath and launched into my explanation. 'First, Directing (S1): in this case the leader provides clear and detailed directions on how the job is to be done but a low level of supportive behaviour. This approach is used when the employee lacks or may have lost competency but is enthusiastic and committed to the task in hand. S2, Coaching, involves providing high levels of both direction and support. It's used where the employee has little experience or competence in doing the task and therefore lacks or may have lost commitment. Thirdly, the Supporting (S3) approach involves using low levels of direction and a high level of supportive behaviour demonstrated by the leader. This is used where the employee is competent to carry out the task but lacks self-confidence or motivation. And, finally, Delegating (S4), where there is a low level of both directive and supportive behaviour displayed by the leader. This is used when the employee is both competent to carry out the task and has the motivation and self-confidence to do it successfully.'

'**Good. Of course, to be able to use this approach effectively, the leader has to analyse the follower's competency and commitment as they relate to each new task. This is time-consuming and implies that the leader has to know the strengths, weaknesses and abilities of each member of staff they deal with.**'

'I think that is one of its weaknesses.' I said. 'As a middle manager with just a few staff, I found the approach really useful when I first learnt it. But a principal in a large comprehensive or college wouldn't have the detailed knowledge of each member that is required to apply this approach effectively. Besides, it would take too long to get around to each member of staff. For these reasons, I've always thought that it was an ideal tool for middle managers but not much use for senior managers/leaders.'

'**I agree with you to a certain extent, but I wouldn't rule out its use across the school. If the principal has analysed the collective strengths and weaknesses of her staff accurately, they will be able to predict how they will react to a particular threat or opportunity. They can then provide to the whole school the required levels of direction and support. But I do agree that it works best on a one-to-one basis.**'

'One thing that I think is misleading about the theory is that it's very easy to think that, as members of staff gain experience, they move from needing high direction and high support to low direction and low support. In reality, it is entirely possible for the member of staff to require no direction and no support for a job on Friday but require high direction and high support for a new task on Monday,' I said.

'**You're quite right. You can't assume that staff move from requiring high direction and support to the position where they need low support and low direction over time. It's not developmental in that sense. Every new task requires a reappraisal of the employee's abilities and needs. Even so, I do think that situational theory is an approach that any new manager or leader should consider, if for no other reason than it requires them to think about their staff. Unlike trait, style and contingency theory, situational theory** is prescriptive. It says "this is how you should lead". It tells the new leader what to do, and how to do it. It's also practical and easy to understand and implement.'

'I read somewhere that, when this approach was used with teachers, it was found that the theory worked well with newly qualified teachers, who preferred principals to have a highly structured leadership style, but that the performance of more experienced teachers was unaffected.'

'We're back to the idea of the structure of the task, its complexity and the level of freedom that members of staff expect to have in how they complete their work. In the case of teachers and other professionals, it also has something to do with professional pride and expectations. The concept that underpins every profession is that, once inducted into the profession, you should become autonomous and therefore free to decide how to complete a piece of work without outside interference.'

'So you still think, despite what you said about managerialism and performativity, that teachers are autonomous professionals?' I asked mischievously, wondering how Martin would wriggle out of his apparent self-contradiction.

'Not really. OfSTED and every government since 1979 have eaten away at our professional independence – if we ever had it. Everyone thinks they know better than us. And they base this firm belief on the fact that they once went to school. You'd never get patients believing that they know better than their doctor just because they spent a month in hospital. But, and it's an important but, teachers still get to exercise professional discretion in their own classroom. Even if they do change their teaching approach when OfSTED is watching!'

'There speaks an old disillusioned romantic,' I said.

'Not so much of the old if you don't mind. Before we end for the day, there is one caveat that I would like to make about situational leadership. McGrath did a piece of research in a university faculty some years ago, and he found that several of the managers there used a form of situational leadership. But many staff he spoke to saw their manager's willingness to spend time with specific staff as a sign of favouritism. They didn't realise that the manager was providing support to weaker, less experienced staff. They failed to understand that the reason the manager spent less time with them was because she had faith and confidence in them!'

'What are we doing next time?' I asked.

'**I want to look at leader member exchange (LMX) and transactional leadership theory (TLX).**

> ### Nat's reflection
>
> **22 October**
>
> Of all the leadership theories, situational is the one I know most about. It's also the only one that I have consciously applied in practice. I'm comfortable with it. For that reason, I need to be careful that I don't use it exclusively and ignore useful approaches and insights contained in other theories.
>
> Regardless of what Martin says about how you can apply situational theory to a group, I still think that it's most effective when you know your staff well and you can deal with each person individually. It's ideal for middle managers; unfortunately, I'll have to leave it behind when I'm in charge of the whole tomalley. Or will I? I could apply it to the members of my senior management team! I'd have to be careful and not excite their professional sensibilities, but in certain circumstances and with just a bit of adaption I could make it work. I need to give this a bit more thought.
>
> Certainly, it's an approach that I should encourage my team and subject leaders to use. I'd better check out how many of them have heard of, or been trained in, situational leadership. If there is enough demand, I could arrange for a trainer to deliver a session on one of the training days.

Space for your notes

Prompts

- Do you have any staff that report to you? If so, what approach do you use to manage and lead them?
- What leadership approaches does your line manager apply when dealing with you?

Record of tutorial

Summary notes from tutorial held on 20 October

- Style theory deals with how leaders act.
- Two categories of behaviour have been identified. Typically, concern for the task has been described as autocratic, restrictive, non-participative, initiating, structured or production-oriented. Personnel-oriented behaviours have been variously described as person-centred, democratic, permissive, consideration behaviours or employee orientation.
- The Ohio State University suggested that the two types of behaviour existed on a single continuum and the leader was required to emphasise one at the expense of the other.
- Michigan State University argued that there were two independent continua and that the leader could choose to emphasise both task and personnel behaviours or any mix of the two that she wished.
- Blake and Mouton suggest that the best mix is high/high, but Martin argues that there are natural peaks and troughs in the work cycle and the leader should adapt her style accordingly.

- Style theory appears to have links with McGregor's X and Y theory of management. X style managers believe that staff have to be constantly monitored to ensure that they work. Y style managers believe that staff want to work and that the manager should create the appropriate environment for them to work in.
- Likert identified four styles of leadership: these he described as exploitive/authoritarian, benevolent/authoritarian, consultative and participative. The first two are broadly task-oriented approaches and the last two personnel-oriented approaches.
- Goleman identified six styles of leadership: coercive, authoritarian, affiliative, democratic, pacesetting and coaching. Again, the first three can be seen as broadly task-oriented approaches and the last three personnel-oriented.
- Style theory's major weakness is that it is unable to identify which style is best in what situation. However, it does appear that a task-centred approach is most successful when an organisation is doing either very well or very badly.
- Hay McBer identified that education leaders tend to use a more authoritarian style of leadership than executives in the private sector who preferred a more pacesetting, people-centred approach.
- Contingency theory combines style theory with consideration of the context within which leaders operate.
- Within contingency theory the context is determined as either favourable or unfavourable by evaluation of three interacting factors:
  - the leader's relationship with the staff
  - how highly structured the task is that staff perform
  - the leader's power to reward or punish staff
- The most favourable position for the leader is where they have good relations with the staff, the task is highly structured and they are free to reward or punish staff with minimum constraints. The worst position is where they have poor relations, the task is unstructured and they can't reward or punish staff as they think appropriate. There are a further six possible combinations of the factors.
- As the theory is personality based, it assumes that the leader is unable to change the way they behave and that, therefore, if they find themselves in a position which is unsatisfactory, they should seek to re-engineer the context rather than seek to change their behaviour.
- The theory offers no suggestions as to how re-engineering might be achieved.

- Contingency theory is predictive in that, if the employers have a leadership profile of an employee, they should be able to predict what types of situations she is likely to be most successful in.
- The theory does not expect a leader to be successful in every situation. However, beyond suggesting that an unsuccessful leader should be moved to a context more suitable to their style, it says little about what to do when a leader is found wanting.
- John Adair's model of leadership, which emphasises task, group and individual needs, is similar to contingency theory in that it looks at the situation a leader finds herself in, but in this instance suggests that where there is a mismatch the leader should change their approach and not seek to re-engineer the situation/context.
- Situational theory was developed by Blanchard. It examines the interaction between the situational variables (the member of staff's competency to perform a task and their commitment or confidence to perform the task) and the leader's behaviour.
- Essentially, situational theory suggests that the leader should use one of four approaches with staff.
- Each of the four approaches is made up of directive and supportive behaviours. It is the precise mix of these behaviours that gives rise to the four styles available. These are:
  - directing, which involves high direction and low support;
  - coaching, which involves high direction and high support;
  - supporting, which involves high support and low direction;
  - delegation, which involves low support and low direction.
- The theory is especially useful for middle managers and leaders who have a small number of staff reporting to them whom they know well.
- Situational theory requires the leader to analyse the strengths and weaknesses of their staff and to provide appropriate support as required. It is a prescriptive theory in that it tells the leader how to lead.
- Situational theory appears to work best with staff that are relatively inexperienced.
- See handout on page 105 for an outline of the strengths and weaknesses of each theory.

Implications of learning for my leadership style

OK, how am I going to use these three theories? Let's start with style theory. I want to be supportive of staff. I want them to feel that I care and that they can raise any issue with me. But I also want them to realise that I expect them to be professional and perform their duties to a high standard. To achieve this I need to build a culture of support and mutual respect among staff, along with a commitment to high standards and getting the job done. That's not going to be easy. But I can make a start by demonstrating my concern and support for all staff by entering into a genuine dialogue with them. Listening to their concerns and problems and trying to resolve them. But at the same time demanding that they perform to a high standard and meet deadlines. It is possible to be firm, fair and supportive. The difficulty is in being consistent. Once I start to use this approach, I have to maintain it and apply it to all staff equally.

Contingency theory is useful. It doesn't tell me how to manage; rather, it gives me the tools to analyse the position I find myself in as a leader. Just knowing that will help me to devise a strategy that will improve or consolidate my position as leader. Once I know where I stand, I can adopt the most appropriate leadership style or approach to achieve my objectives.

I've used situational theory in the past with some success. Therefore, I need to guard against becoming overreliant upon it. I also need to consider if I want to use it with experienced staff. If they see through what I am doing, it's likely that their professional pride will be injured and they will resent being treated in such a way. Perhaps what I need to do is adapt the approach. When discussing their work and the tasks I ask them to do, I must make it clear that I am happy to provide support or guidance if they need it. The problem is that many people see asking for help as a sign of weakness. If I'm going to use this approach, then I have to demonstrate that I don't support such a view. The best way I can do that is by demonstrating my own willingness to ask for help and support when I need it. There's too much macho management knocking around. Our inability to say 'I don't know' or ask for advice and help probably accounts for half of all the mistakes that management make. And trying to maintain the façade of being the all-wise, all-knowing leader probably results in more heart attacks from stress than any other factor at work.

I know how to use situational theory with one member of staff. I need to think about how I can apply it to groups. Essentially, it is still about analysing where the group is in terms of competency and commitment. Hang on, I've just had an idea. I might not have the time to analyse each group but the group leader will know about the group's strengths, weaknesses and needs. I could use their knowledge to determine my approach.

Figure 5.4 Comparison of trait, style, contingency and situational theory

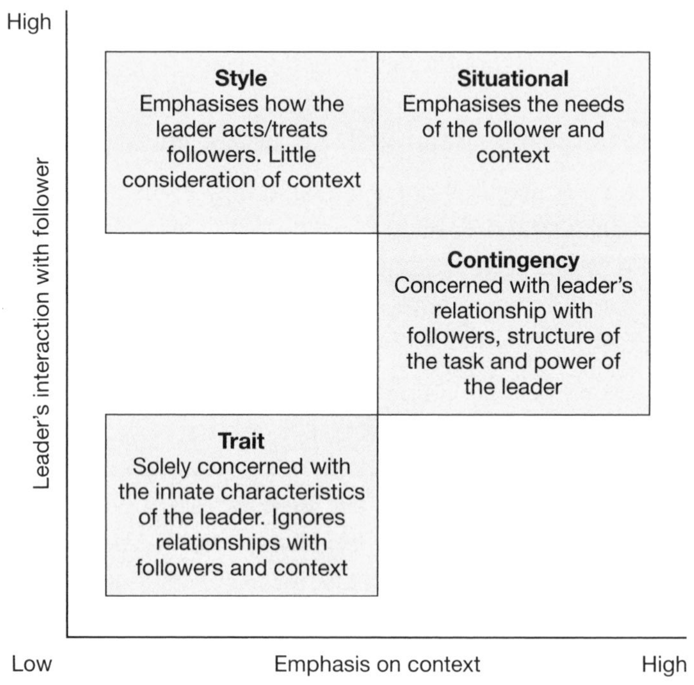

Handout

Table 5.3 Comparison of the strengths and weaknesses of style, contingency and situational leadership theories

Strengths	Style	Contingency	Situational
Changes the focus of research from consideration of the leader's character traits to how they interact with followers.	X	X	X
Basic tenets supported by a wide range of empirical studies.	X	X	
Establishes the idea that the leader must mix their desire for completion of task with support and care for employees.	X		X
Provides leaders with an insight into how others see them.	X		
Requires leaders to think about the context/situation in which leadership is exercised.		X	X
A predictive theory that suggests which situations a leader is most likely to be successful in.		X	
Theory recognises that leaders are unlikely to be effective in all situations.		X	
Information on a leader's style allows employers to develop leadership profiles on employees.		X	
Has been found easy to apply in the 'real world'.			X
Frequently used in leadership training.			X
Theory is intuitively attractive. It sounds more like common sense than a theory.	X		X
The principles behind the theory are relatively easy to understand.	X		X
It is a prescriptive theory, e.g. it tells leaders what to do in a situation.			X
It emphasises the need for flexibility from the leader.	-		X
It reminds the leader to treat every encounter with a follower differently based upon the task at hand.			X

Weaknesses	Style	Contingency	Situational
Research has failed to identify how the theory impacts on performance and attitudes of staff.	X	X	X
Research has failed to find the most appropriate style to apply in all situations.	X	X	
It remains unclear if a high emphasis on both the task and staff is the most desirable approach.	X		
It fails to explain why leaders with certain styles are more effective in certain situations.	X		
Impractical to use in the real world. Organisations can't keep moving a leader until they find the correct 'situation' for him/her.		X	
Fails to explain what leaders should do when there is a mismatch between their skills and a particular situation. Because leadership is seen as a personality issue, it does not suggest that the leader amend their style to suit the situation.		X	
Where the leader is unsuccessful the theory implies that the situation be re-engineered to suit the leader. But it provides no advice on how it should be done.		X	
Because the leader needs to spend more time with some members of staff than others, they can be accused of favouritism.			X
Only a few research studies have been conducted into the principles that underpin the theory.			X
Not clear what the terms 'competence' and 'commitment' mean.			X
Not clear how followers move through the developmental stages or if they do.			X
Unclear if the theory can be applied to all followers. Does it work better with staff that have routine jobs? Does it work with professional staff who may resent being given direction?			X
The questionnaire used in conjunction with the theory only takes into account the four specific parameters of situational leadership (directing, coaching, supporting, and delegating); there are other parameters.			X

Additional information on the issues covered by this tutorial can be found at/in:

- www.pearsoned.com/mcgrathandcoles
- www.businessballs.com
- Cole, G.A. (2004) *Management Theory and Practice*, 6th edn. London: Thomson Learning.
- Handy, C. (1993) *Understanding Organisations*. London: Penguin Books.
- Northouse, P.G. (2007) *Leadership Theory and Practice*, 4th edn. London: Sage.

Leader member exchange (LMX) and transactional theory (TLX)

Aim of tutorial

By the end of the tutorial you will be able to explain the differences and similarities between leader member exchange (LMX) and transactional leadership theory (TLX) and identify the strengths and weaknesses of each. You will also continue to identify and develop your own preferred leadership style.

Contents

- LMX theory described and defined
- Examples of LMX theory in practice
- TLX theory described and defined
- Examples of TLX in practice
- Links between LMX, TLX and Maslow's hierarchy of needs
- Strengths and weaknesses of LMX and TLX

Nat's reflection

27 October

Martin emailed me yesterday and said that he would be leaving early today. Apparently he's got 'hot tickets' for a play in London. He gave me the choice of either delaying the session until next week or having a shorter tutorial. I've always found that regular attendance at sessions is the best way to stay interested in and connected to a course. This is probably even more important when the sessions are voluntary and there is no final assessment to keep me motivated. So I settled for a shorter session.

I wonder which play Marin is off to see?

Review of tutorial

Martin was at his desk when I arrived and although he was dressed casually, as always, in an open-neck shirt, v-neck jumper and dark slacks, he looked smarter than usual.

'Newly pressed trousers,' I said. 'It must be a very special play.'

'Indeed it is. My daughter phoned last night. She has a spare ticket for "Cat on a Hot Tin Roof". I have to get to London by 6.30.'

'Who's in it?'

'It's the all-black production with James Earl Jones as Big Daddy.'

'The voice of Darth Vader,' I said sonorously.

'The very same. So let's crack on and I can catch my train. I'd planned to look at transactional, transformational and charismatic leadership today. But instead I suggest that we concentrate on transactional leadership (TLX), and to make it worth your while coming we can review leader member exchange (LMX) as well.'

'LMX? I've not heard of that one.'

'It's a fairly new theory but I'm willing to bet you've come across it in every job you've ever had, even if you didn't know what it's called.'

'Sounds interesting,' I said doubtfully.

'According to Richmon and Allison, LMX "examines the reciprocal influence relationship between leaders and individual subordinates. Each exchange relationship is unique because the role of the subordinate is mutually defined". That's a bit of a mouthful but essentially LMX is concerned with the relationship that exists between the leader and each individual follower. Two types of followers are identified. Northouse explains that those in the 'in-group' have negotiated an expanded role or range of duties, compared with the 'out-group' that comprises staff that work to their job description. In return for assuming more responsibilities, the in-group members enjoy a special relationship with the leader that is characterised by the high level of trust and confidence she places in them. They are considered more dependable, moti-vated and communicative than the out-group members.'

'Hmm, I'm not sure I like the sound of LMX.'

'Well, before you make up your mind, let me continue. Unlike the previous theories we've discussed which, with the possible exception of situational theory, are all concerned with leaders, LMX focuses on the quality of the one-to-one relationship between the leader and each follower. Basically, the theory suggests that it's the leader's responsibility to build strong and mutu-ally supportive relations with each follower.'

'And how do they do that?' I asked doubtfully.

'Well, in the words of Graen and Uhl-Bien, they attempt to form a dyadic relationship with each follower that is based upon the follower taking on an enhanced role. If the follower is willing to take on this expanded role, they become members of the "in group"; if they don't, they remain in the "out group".

'Dyadic?' I queried.

'It means a pair or couple: in this case, the leader and follower. Its use also implies that there exist free and open channels of communication between the pair.'

'It still sounds unethical to me, with some people being treated better than others by the leader.'

'Possibly. But the theory stipulates that all those interested in being a member of the in-group should be offered the opportunity to become a member of the in-group. This, it's claimed, addresses any charges of discrimination or favouritism.'

'So what do the members of the in-group get for working harder than the out-group?'

'In-group members don't necessarily work harder; they're just willing to be more flexible, work beyond their job description and take on tasks that are outside their job description. In return, they receive more information from the leader about what is happening in the organisation and enjoy greater access to and influence with the leader. This obviously increases their status as they are seen as having the ear of the leader. The fact that the follower is seen as a dependable and committed member of staff has advantages when promotions come around.'

'And what are the advantages to the organisation?'

'According to research, the organisation benefits from a lower rate of staff turnover and a more enthusiastic workforce. Such a workforce is more committed to the organisation's future and is willing to work with greater enthusiasm in order to achieve the organisation's goals than the norm.'

'It still sounds as if everyone except those in the out-group is a winner. How do you become a member of the in-group?'

'Graen and Uhl-Bien suggest that to become a member of the in-group the follower moves through three phases. In stage one (stranger) the follower is part of the out-group. They work according to their job description but are monitored by the leader who wishes to see if they have the flexibility to become in-group members. Stage two (acquaintance) starts when the leader offers the follower the opportunity to work outside their job description with the inducement that this will benefit their career. If accepted, the relationship between the leader and follower starts to change. The level and frequency of communication between the two increases and the leader becomes something of a mentor to the follower. But the follower is still not a full member of the in-group. Stage two is a time of exploration and testing on both sides and either party can terminate the "new relationship".'

'So it's like a courtship.'

'You could say that. Stage three (mature partnership) occurs when the follower convinces the leader that they have the commitment and skills required to work beyond their job description. This change in relationship is indicated by a high degree of trust, responsibility, loyalty and reciprocity on both sides.'

'It still strikes me as favouritism dressed up as a theory in order to make it respectable. And if the leader is unethical, the courtship can become a seduction with promises of extra rewards for extra work,' I said with feeling.

'It sounds to me as if you've spent some time in an out-group.'

'How did you guess? You're right. I've seen in-groups in action. My experience has been that membership of the in-group is not based upon a list of extended duties but on the personal relationship or history that exists between leader and follower. For example, in one school the in-group comprised those who went drinking with the principal on a Friday night. Needless to say the principal rarely paid for a drink. While in one college it was those members of the senior management team that smoked that were the in-group. They used to hold impromptu smokers' meetings on the steps of the college, where they took major decisions about the future of the college without reference to the rest of the senior management team.'

'And I take it that you didn't want to take up drinking or smoking?'

'I had a perfectly good professional relationship with both groups, and I have never just worked to my job description, but it's not in my nature to spend hours and hours with people socially on the off chance that it will benefit my career.'

'Such cronyism as you describe is a corruption of LMX theory. But I'm not so naive as to claim that what you say doesn't happen. There's the very real danger with LMX that the out-group can feel that they are excluded and treated like second-class citizens. This can be very harmful for any organisation. Remember what Handy (Tutorial 2) said about negative power. People who feel slighted or excluded can cause a lot of problems in any organisation. But the charge that LMX is elitist and inequitable is countered by the assertion that the leader should seek to achieve this special relationship with all of their followers and not just a selected few. Despite your reservations, I personally think that LMX theory remains an important element in understanding organisational relationships. After all, just about every professional relationship we enter into has an element of exchange in it. Yes, we come to work for a variety of reasons, but one of them is that we receive payment in exchange for our labour. Here, have a look at my handout on the strengths and weaknesses of LMX and transactional theory and see if you change your mind (see handout page 121).'

Nat's reflection

28 October

I may not have heard of LMX but I have certainly seen it in action. Unfortunately I've only ever seen corrupt versions of it. Is it possible to consciously use the theory and not end up with charges of favouritism and even discrimination being levelled at you? I don't know.

Certainly, if I were to use it widely, there would be a risk that the out-group would become demotivated and resentful. Such a situation could have serious consequences at the time of an OfSTED inspection, which would present the ideal opportunity for disgruntled staff to exact their revenge when asked about management and leadership in the organisation.

That said, there are real advantages to giving staff the opportunity to work outside their job description. People grow bored and need to be stretched, and asking them to undertake an unusual piece of work can motivate them. It's also a good way of developing staff and checking out if they are ready to take on additional responsibilities before they are promoted.

So, maybe, instead of seeking to create an in-group, I should concentrate on providing all staff with opportunities to stretch themselves. I can also avoid charges of favouritism, by consciously avoiding the creation of meetings and events to which only the select few are invited.

Space for your notes

Prompts

- Have you ever worked in an organisation where there were clear in- and out-groups? How did that make you feel?
- How might you use your knowledge of LMX theory as: (a) a leader and (b) a follower?

Review of tutorial

'So what do you know about transactional leadership (TLX)?' Martin asked.

'I think it can be summed up by the old saying "If you scratch my back I'll scratch yours". The idea is that the leader uses inducements or threats to the get the follower to do what they want. For example, "If you do this for me, I'll give you Friday afternoon off". Or "If you don't do this job, I'll make sure that you have to attend every parents' evening in the spring term". Of course these offers and/or threats are always wrapped up in appropriate language.'

'That's a pretty good summary. The term "transactional leadership" was coined by Burns and, as you say, it describes the process by which a leader "buys" compliance from the follower in exchange for either rewards, such as pay or recognition (constructive transactions), or the imposition of penalties such as "naming and shaming" or demotion (corrective transactions). The theory is underpinned by self-interest on the part of both the leader and follower and does not involve either party in the emotional or intellectual stimulation that is involved in transformational relationships. We'll look at transformational theory (TL) next time. But, just as a general principle, do you think that a leader should be free to use the full range of different leadership theories that are available to them to achieve their objectives?'

'On balance, I think a leader should be willing to use any theory provided it's ethical.'

'I agree, but there are many people who have the idea that if you are a transformational leader you shouldn't dirty your hands using TLX. They probably got the idea from Burns who conceptualised transactional and transformational leadership as residing at the opposite ends of the same continuum. But Bass saw them as existing on two different continua.'

'It sounds like a replay of the style theory debate between Ohio State University and Michigan University (see Tutorial 5).'

'Indeed it does. Middlehurst argues that Bass's interpretation is the most useful as it allows transformational leaders to act in transactional ways when required. She reports that a number of commentators have suggested that a transactional approach is particularly appropriate in academic and other professional institutions. But what she is probably describing is the process whereby professionals of equal or near equal status help each other out, rather than any exchange of rewards or punishments.'

'I wouldn't be so sure. A colleague of mine once said that the only thing that united teaching staff was a common grievance over parking. Academic staff are just as venal as any other group of employees,' I said.

'There speaks a true cynic after my own heart. To achieve their aims, transactional leaders clarify the role and task requirements of their followers and "buy" compliance in exchange for either rewards, such as pay or recognition (constructive transactions), or the imposition of penalties such as 'naming and shaming' or demotion (corrective transactions).'

'From what you say, it seems that leaders who exhibit a task-oriented style of leadership would be happy to use transactional leadership to get things done (Tutorial 5),' I said.

'I think that's probably true. They are task-focused and are generally willing to use whatever tools are available to them to achieve their objective. It's a generalisation, but many transactional leaders tend to stress the impersonal aspects of performance, such as the achievement of aims and objectives. In doing so, they often demonstrate a strong sense of commitment to the organisation and a willingness to conform to organisational norms and values.'

'So, in the terms of Gleeson and Shain, they would be willing compliers (see Tutorial 1) or at least strategic compliers.'

'That's probably a fair assumption. Hell, is that the time?' said Martin looking at his watch. 'I have to be going. Here's a diagram that I have been working on that links some of the theories we have discussed and will discuss in the next two tutorials (see Figure 6.1 page 120). **See what you can make of it and read up on transformational leadership for next week. I'll bring you back a programme.'**

Nat's reflection

29 October

Listening to the tape, I realise that there is an inconsistency in my leadership philosophy. I told Martin that a leader should use any theory that will help her to achieve her objectives. Why, then, am I unwilling to use LMX? It's probably because I feel it's discriminatory, with certain people being preferred over others. But if that's the case, why am I happy to use TLX and reward or coerce people into doing certain tasks? It's probably because TLX involves negotiating individual deals with people on an **ad hoc** basis and not the creation of semi-fixed categories of staff, some of whom are rewarded for just being members of the group and not for specific actions.

All teachers, not just leaders, use TLX regularly. With colleagues, it can be 'If you cover for me today, I'll teach your class on Thursday.' Or in class, 'If you complete the exercise correctly, you can use the spare time to work on your own project.' And I've certainly used TLX as a leader. It's the oil that enables the machine to keep going: for example, 'We need to get these returns off today. If you work late tonight you can have Friday afternoon off. So I have no problems using a bit of 'bribery and coercion' when it suits me.

That said, I've never really thought much about the **ethics** of leadership. Just how far would I be willing to go to get the job done? I would like to think that I would never harm or exploit people to achieve my objectives. Nor would I ever ask them to do something that was against their conscience. But I'm not certain where I'd draw the line. I'll mention this to Martin and see if we can discuss ethics at a future session.

Space for your notes

Prompts

● Think of occasions when a manager has used TLX to get you to do something. How did it make you feel?

● Think of occasions when you have used TLX with colleagues or learners to achieve what you wanted. How do you think that person felt?

Record of tutorial

Summary notes from tutorial held on 27 October

● LMX emphasises the reciprocal relationship between the leader and follower. Each relationship is unique.

● LMX creates an in-group comprised of followers who are willing to work outside the requirements laid down in their job description and out-group members who continue to work to their job description.

● LMX aims to create a series of excellent relationships between the leader and each follower that is characterised by high levels of trust and mutual respect. But inevitably those who remain outside the in-group have a less rich relationship with the leader.

● Membership of the in-group should be open to all those that are willing to work outside their job description and take on an enhanced role in the school or college. Membership should not be restricted on the basis of the leader's personal bias or prejudice.

- Members of the in-group enjoy the benefits of enhanced status, ready access to the leader, and the opportunity to express their views and opinions on issues affecting them and their staff before any decision is made.
- The benefits to the organisation include lower staff turnover, a core group of flexible, highly committed and enthusiastic staff.
- However, use of LMX can lead to the out-group feeling resentful, demotivated and restless. This can result in individuals exercising negative power: for example, by undermining the leader or sabotaging new initiatives.
- While LMX seeks to be ethical by insisting that membership of the in-group should be open to all and solely dependent on the followers' willingness to work beyond their job description, it is nevertheless open to the charge of cronyism, with membership of the in-group being dependent on whom you socialise with, personality or shared histories.
- TLX sees leadership as a series of negotiated transactions between the leader and follower.
- TLX addresses many of the lower level wants that Maslow identified in his hierarchy of needs, such as the need for shelter, food and safety, all of which are dependent upon or enhanced by earning a living.
- TLX and transformational leadership do not reside at opposite ends of the same continuum, as suggested by Burns, but on two continua, as argued by Bass. This enables the transformational leader to use TLX when appropriate.
- Middlehurst suggests that TLX is widely used in academic and professional organisations. In such situations any transactions undertaken are likely to take place between equals or near equals and be similar to the exchange of favours.
- TLX leaders are usually focused on task completion, and therefore their style of leadership can often be described as task/autocratic.

Implications of learning for my leadership style

I don't care what Martin says, I'm still uneasy about the idea of differential treatment for staff based upon an unwritten agreement between myself and individual followers. It offends my sense of fair and equitable treatment for all. I can see that LMX has the potential to make the staff feel important, involved and valuable. If I can achieve that, I will have a highly motivated and committed workforce. So what should I do? The obvious answer would appear to be to create a culture that enables all staff to feel as if they belong to the in-group while ensuring that there is no discernible out-group. Easier said than done. But maybe that should be my vision for the relationship that I want to have with all my followers: a relationship based on mutual respect, loyalty to the organisation and a commitment to go the extra mile in order to do a good job. If I am going to try to achieve that, then staff recruitment, selection and retention are key areas for me to concentrate on when I become principal. I need to ensure that I recruit the type of people who would respond to 'partnership working'.

As for transactional leadership, we all do it to some extent. How many times have I negotiated with a member of staff to cover for someone or take on added responsibilities in return for a reward of some kind? Very often the person doesn't want a financial reward. Recognition or a simple thank-you is often enough. So how does that differ from LMX ethically? Let me see. It's a one-off arrangement, not a systematic approach to how I manage and lead, and acceptance or refusal on the part of the follower does not mean that I cast them out into the dark regions of the out-group. No, transactional leadership has existed since time immemorial and embodies the give and take between management and staff that is essential to the smooth running of any organisation. So it stays in my leadership arsenal.

Figure 6.1 Maslow's hierarchy of needs, with links to leader member exchange and transactional, transformational and distributed leadership theory

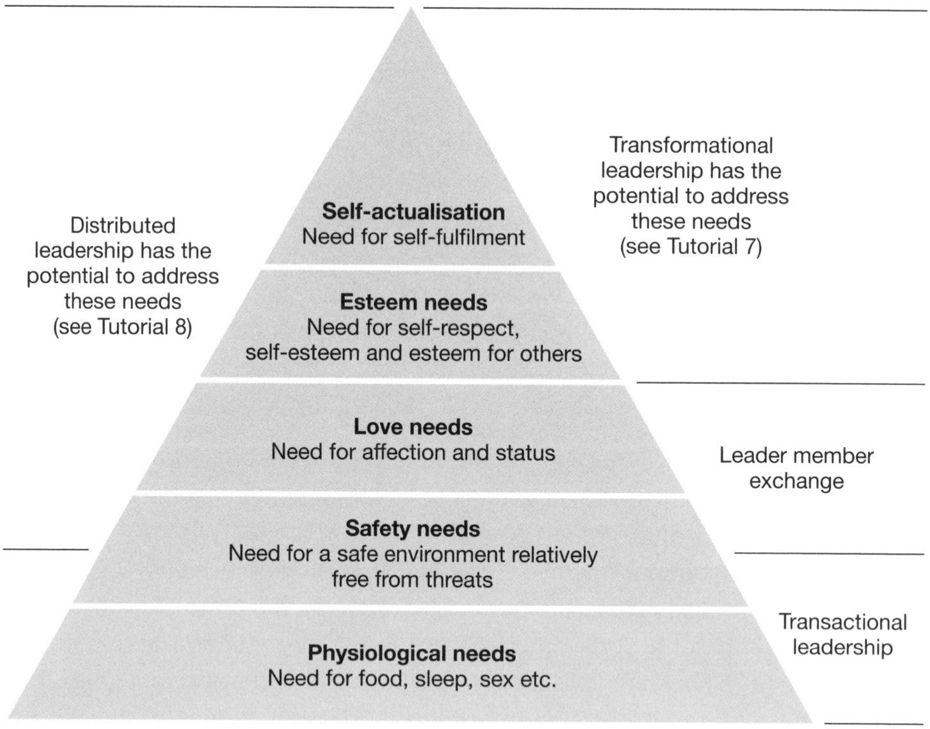

Transformational leadership has the potential to address these needs (see Tutorial 7)

Distributed leadership has the potential to address these needs (see Tutorial 8)

Self-actualisation
Need for self-fulfilment

Esteem needs
Need for self-respect, self-esteem and esteem for others

Love needs
Need for affection and status

Leader member exchange

Safety needs
Need for a safe environment relatively free from threats

Physiological needs
Need for food, sleep, sex etc.

Transactional leadership

Note: The links between Maslow's and the other leadership theories discussed in this book, but not listed above, are less obvious but you may wish to consider to what extent, if any, they exist.

Handout

Table 6.1 Strengths and weaknesses of LMX and transactional leadership theories

Note: It is entirely possible for a factor to be simultaneously both a strength and a weakness.

Strengths of LMX
A descriptive theory that reflects the reality of most organisations, it therefore has credibility with leaders.
Intuitively, it makes sense as it resonates with our experience of working life and is relatively easy to implement.
Unlike other theories that are concerned with what the leader does or the situation in which leadership is exercised, LMX emphasises the relationship between the leader and individual follower.
LMX highlights the need for good communications between leader and follower.
Potentially, it guards against the leader's biases as inclusion in the in-group should be based upon assessable criteria (ability to work outside job description) rather than personal preference based upon sex, age, ethnicity, personality.
Research has linked the use of LMX to improved organisational performance. However, what cannot be known is whether this improvement would have been achieved or been even greater if LMX was not used.

Weaknesses of LMX
The theory is descriptive and does not explain how the leader can create high-quality relationships with individual members of staff.
LMX can create resentment among out-group members who can become demotivated and exercise negative power in terms of disruptive behaviour.
Can be considered unfair and discriminatory as it creates two groups of unequal status.
Can be corrupted and become cronyism.
While it is claimed that research has linked the use of LMX to improved organisational performance, it is impossible to say whether this improvement would have been achieved or been even greater if LMX was not used.

Strengths of TLX
A descriptive theory that reflects what occurs in all organisations, therefore it has credibility with leaders.
Intuitively, it makes sense as it resonates with our experience of working life and is easy to understand and apply.
Can be applied in a wide variety of situations and setting.
The leader is able to choose from a very wide range of constructive transactions (rewards) or corrective transactions (punishments), only some of which are financial, to achieve their objectives.
Can be used in conjunction with other leadership theories: e.g. style, contingency, situational, LMX and transformational.

Weaknesses of TLX
TLX enables the leader to exercise considerable power over the follower by either granting or denying favours or resources.
Unlike transformational leadership, TLX does not address the followers' higher needs in terms of finding fulfilment and meaning in their work.
There is a danger that a leader may rely upon corrective transactions to achieve their objectives, which can lead to an oppressive and bullying work environment.
Is not available to leaders who have no formal position in the organisation and therefore can't engage in constructive or corrective offers.
Can cause resentment when staff see others being rewarded while they receive no reward or suffer corrective action.

Additional information on the issues covered by this tutorial can be found at/in:

- www.pearsoned.com/mcgrathandcoles
- www.businessballs.com
- **Northouse, P.G.** (2007) *Leadership Theory and Practice*, 4th edn. London: Sage.

Charismatic (CL) and transformational leadership (TL)

Aim of tutorial

By the end of the tutorial you will be able to outline the difference between these two theories and explain why transformational leadership has become the theory of choice for the public sector.

Contents

- Charismatic and transformational leadership defined
- Features of charismatic leadership
- Why charismatic leadership is not the same as transformational leadership.
- The origins of transformational leadership (Burns and Bass)
- Later developments in transformational leadership (Bennis and Nanus, Tichy and De Vanna, and Kouzes and Posner)
- Applying charismatic and transformational leadership in the public sector
- Strengths and weaknesses of charismatic and transformational leadership

Nat's reflection

3 November

I wonder if the play and James Earl Jones were as good as Martin anticipated. I saw the Pogues a few years ago and was desperately disappointed by their tame performance. They were just going through the motions with none of the glorious mayhem that they were known for in their pomp. But then, it's always a risk to see our heroes in the flesh: after all, they are only human and can easily fail to live up to our idealised image of them. A bit like leaders, really. Look closely and they appear all too human.

It's probably because I see the human weaknesses inherent in all leaders that I'm not a fan of charismatic and transformational leadership. From what I've read, both theories seem to put leaders on a pedestal. And you just know that eventually they are going to disappoint you. You only have to look at the great figures of history to see the contradictions that were inherent in their characters. Even Lincoln, the great emancipator, admitted that if he had to choose between freeing the slaves and saving the Union, he would have saved the Union. His vision was for a United States of America, not emancipation.

Transformational leadership has become the leadership theory of choice in education in recent years. It seems that every job advert for a principal requires the successful applicant be inspiring, passionate and with a clear vision for education, the implication being that such people are hanging about on every street corner waiting to be picked up. So if I'm going to make principal, I need to know more about transformational leadership and how it differs from charismatic leadership. That way I will be able to 'talk the talk' at interview! How cynical is that?

Review of tutorial

Martin was rummaging in his desk when I entered. Looking up, he smiled.

'How was it?' I asked.

With a bashful grin he replied, '**Marvellous performance. I even spoke to the great man!**'

'You spoke to James Earl Jones?' I said with astonishment.

Martin laughed at my expression. '**It was no big deal,**' he said. '**I got to the theatre far too early and went for a walk. He was standing outside getting a breath of air. I ran across the road, almost got knocked down, and asked for his autograph like some star-struck 15-year-old.**'

'You spoke to him! I do hope you didn't say "May the force be with you".'

'**Now that you mention it… Anyway I got one for you,**' he said and handed me an advertising flyer for the play signed by James Earl Jones along the margin.'

I was speechless and held it like a holy relic.

'**You can buy me a coffee later and I'll tell you all about it, but for now what do you know about charismatic and transformational leadership?**'

'I reread Bennis and Nanus's book *Leaders*. I really liked the pen portraits of leaders that take up the first half of the book but I'm less impressed by the theories discussed in part two. If I'm honest, I could do with reading that section again. But I am aware that since they wrote their book in the mid-90s transformational leadership has become the dominant approach in education. We're constantly told by the government that education needs more principals with vision and an ability to energise and motivate the staff behind it. As for charismatic leadership I have my doubts.'

'**Do I detect a hint of cynicism?**' I inclined my head and Martin continued, '**First, it's important to recognise that although the two theories share certain characteristics they are not the same. Essentially, the charismatic leaders have extraordinary qualities which draw people to them. Like iron filings to a magnet. Think of Richard Branson. But they don't always provide a vision for their followers. Transformational leaders, however, seek to appeal to their followers' higher order values and morals and to encourage them to seek self-actualisation by transcending their own self-interests for the greater good of the team or organisation. Prime examples of transformational leaders are Martin Luther King and Nelson Mandela. They were both charismatic and** transformational: they not only drew people to them but also provided a vision that inspired their followers to achieve staggering results.'

'OK, so what is this magical quality that draws people to charismatic leaders?'

'That's the $64,000 question. If I knew, I'd bottle it. Weber described charisma as being a special personality characteristic possessed by very few. I think it's more likely to be a mixture of qualities, including self-confidence, sociability, an ability to dominate a group, and great communication skills. Good, even great, communication skills are really important because they allow charismatic leaders to connect with their followers. They then reinforce their message by demonstrating in their actions the beliefs, values and morals that they want their followers to emulate and, in doing so, motivate their followers to act in a similar way. To use that awful phrase "they walk the talk".'

'So what's the follower's role in this relationship?' I asked.

'I can see where you're going with this,' Martin replied, 'but I'll play along. Followers are expected to show unquestioning trust and acceptance of the ideology, beliefs and views of the leader. They are encouraged to show their loyalty by identifying with the leader at every opportunity and are obedient to her instructions. There is also usually an emotional element involved in the relationship, with followers showing respect, affection and concern for the leader.'

'And therein lies the problem,' I said. 'Charismatic leadership makes it too easy for unscrupulous people to exploit their followers. There are plenty of con artists in the world of politics, business, religion and, yes, even education that use their skills to draw people into their sphere of influence and then manipulate and use them. If I'm honest, I'm worried that followers of charismatic leaders often leave their critical faculties behind when they embrace the beliefs of such people. In my experience very few people, let alone leaders, are worthy of such unconditional trust.'

'I concede that charismatic leadership can be misused and exploited. But would you agree that, by believing in their followers' abilities and demanding the best from them, charismatic leaders that are ethical can motivate their followers to achieve way beyond what they thought possible and that this achievement increases the followers' self-confidence and self-worth?'

'Yes, I can see that.'

'OK then. Just remember that you need to separate the theory from the people that use it. There is nothing inherently unethical in charismatic leadership. But, as you say, there are plenty of unethical people who use their charisma for their own ends. All the theory seeks to do is describe and explain one form of leadership which we know exists.'

Nat's reflection

4 November

Am I a cynic? Is that why I don't like/trust charismatic leaders? Or is it deeper than that? Is it that at heart I don't trust people, that I always expect them to let me down? Help! I sound like I need a shrink.

I suppose it's just experience. I've worked with some people who were charismatic. They had no difficulty attracting followers. They were fun to be around and they could make you feel special. But generally they were also narcissistic, self-obsessed and entirely untrustworthy. Obviously, not all charismatic leaders are like that, but I think it's safer to be sceptical about such people until such time as you can judge them fairly, based upon their actions and achievements.

What's that instruction that boxing referees give fighters before the start of every fight? ... Oh yeah, 'Defend yourself at all times'. That's not a bad philosophy to have when dealing with a charismatic leader initially.

Space for your notes

Prompts

- Think of a person that you feel is charismatic. It might be someone you worked with or someone in the public eye. What is it about them that makes you think they are charismatic?

- Think of a person you like or who you think is charismatic. To what extent can you separate your feelings for that person when trying to critically evaluate their actions? Do your feelings influence your evaluation?

Review of tutorial

'Turning to transformational leadership, do you think it is necessary for all transformational leaders to be charismatic?'

'Yes and no,' I said, hedging my bets. 'As I said, I read Bennis and Nanus, and, if you look at the pen portraits that they provided of transformational leaders, it's clear that not all of them were particularly charismatic in the sense that they had magnetic personalities and were great orators. However, they were all able to exercise considerable personal influence.'

'Exactly, there is an element of charisma in transformational leadership but it doesn't need to be the dominant characteristic. However, don't underestimate its importance. Gronn, writing in 1996, argues that a degree of charisma is essential to transformational leadership but that charismatic leaders need not be transformational.'

'You mean that charismatic leaders can have the force of personality but not the vision that a transformational leader has.'

'Partly, but there are other considerations as well. Let's go back to the beginning. The theory of transformational leadership was originally mooted by Burns and developed further by Bass. According to Middlehurst, it tries to tap into people's altruistic motivations and personal ideals to achieve the leader's objectives. As we discussed last time, Burns saw transformational leadership residing on the same continuum as transactional leadership and expected that the majority of interactions between leader and follower would be transactional in nature. However, in transformational interactions, Burns believed that leaders could create a connection with the follower that raised the level of motivation and morality of both parties. Key to this was the need for the leader to be attentive to the needs of the followers. Once these had been identified, it was the leader's task to articulate the follower's ambitions and show how these could be satisfied through alignment with and achievement of the team's or organisation's goals. In doing this, the leader helped the follower to grow and move ever closer to achievement of their full potential.'

'So, effectively, the transformational leader tries to indentify the follower's desires, dreams and motives and then uses this knowledge to help them motivate the follower and reach the organisation's objectives,' I said.

'You make it sound so manipulative. It's true that Bass argues that transformational leaders seek to raise their followers' level of consciousness about the importance of work goals and encourages them to transcend their own self-interests for the greater good of the group or organisation. But he suggests that in doing this the followers are able to address their own higher needs. Which leads nicely back to Tutorial 6 and your interesting use of Maslow: it can be said that TL has connections with the higher levels of Maslow's hierarchy of needs.'

'My problem is that, like charismatic leadership, transformational leadership is open to abuse.'

'**You are obsessed with evil doers,**' laughed Martin. '**Bass and Riggio argue that managers, principals and teachers who are only interested in their own self-aggrandisement should be called pseudo-transformational leaders because they are not concerned with the needs of their followers but only interested in power and achievement of their own personal ambitions and desires, regardless of the cost to others.**'

'So we're back to separating the theory from the people that apply it.'

'**Yes. Bass and, later, Bass and Avolio suggested that transformational leaders are engaged in four activities known as the Four Is. The first is that transformational leaders seek to exercise idealised influence (charisma). This is achieved when the followers are drawn to the leader and try to emulate her example. So it is essential that the leader models the behaviour that she wishes to see from her followers, and that her actions demonstrate their commitment to high ethical standards and morals. Because of the image they project, the leader is trusted by the followers.**'

'And this attraction to the leader means that the followers buy into the leader's vision for the organisation,' I said. 'What about the second I?'

'**To exercise inspirational motivation, the leader has to have high expectations of her followers and be able to communicate these expectations to every follower. But the leader does more than communicate her expectations; she makes it clear that she has the utmost faith and confidence in the followers' ability to achieve the targets set. This increases the followers' self-confidence and energises them,**' Martin said.

'I suppose that this energising is important.'

'**Why do you say that?**' Martin asked.

'Because it would make people feel good about themselves and the job they do and this would help create a virtuous circle and emotional attachment to the leader and other members of the team or organisation.'

'**That's exactly what the leader is trying to do – create a self-perpetuating virtuous circle. The third feature is intellectual stimulation. Building on the self-confidence of staff, the leader encourages them to challenge old** ways of doing things and to be creative and innovative in what they do. To achieve this, the TL leader encourages people to challenge their own values and beliefs.'

'That's never an easy thing to do,' I said.

'No, it isn't, and it can be a very uncomfortable experience for the people involved. The final I is individualised consideration. This is based on the leader's willingness to form one-to-one relationships with followers. A bit like the relationship that leaders have with members of the in-group in LMX. The leader actively listens to what followers say and takes on board their suggestions and recommendations when appropriate. She also seeks to develop the follower by giving them opportunities to excel.'

'How would she do this?'

'Well, she might delegate work or encourage the follower to apply for promotions or undertake additional study: basically, whatever will help the follower to grow and develop. Of course that's just one perspective of transformational leadership; there are others: for example, Bennis and Nanus. You said that you had read their book *Leaders*. Can you remember what they said?'

'As I said, what impressed me most were the pen portraits they had of transformational leaders which made up the first half the book. I found the second part fairly confusing.'

'Fair enough. They don't disagree with Burns and Bass; rather, they repackage some of the ideas and make them clearer. They suggest that transformational leaders demonstrate five characteristics. First, they have a clear vision for their organisation that is reasonable, attractive and doable. They are able to explain their vision in such a way that followers are able to see where they fit into it, to identify their role if you like. This gives the follower a sense of personal value and purpose, and encourages them to buy into the leader's vision. Secondly, they shape the organisational culture and promote shared values, meanings and understandings between all the staff. This is important because, if a leader can align their aims with those of their followers, they improve their chances of success exponentially.'

'We're back to Tutorial 2 and the role of the leader in changing and shaping organisational culture.'

'Indeed we are. I'd like to come back to that in a moment. Of course, if you can achieve a shared culture, it can be a very strong unifying force in any organisation. Thirdly, they demonstrate where they stand on issues and are consistent and predictable in how they act, behave and make decisions.'

'And, of course, Goleman (Tutorial 1) argued that staff trust leaders that are consistent and predictable.'

'Precisely. Finally, transformational leaders have no false modesty. They know their strengths and weaknesses. They have a realistic picture of their capabilities and enjoy what Benis and Nanus call positive self-regard. This self-confidence is based on a genuine critical evaluation of their abilities and is communicated to followers, creating in them a feeling of confidence in and respect for the leader.'

Martin paused and appeared to be just about to wind up the session when I asked, 'You mentioned returning to transformational leaders and changing the organisation culture.'

'Oh, yes. Tichy and De Vanna see transformational leaders as change agents. They argue that the process of change requires the creation of a new vision and a road map of how to get there. This is provided by the transformational leader who encourages the breakdown of old structures and ways of doing things and building new ones. What this means is that leading change is intrinsic to the theory of transformational leadership. The very name implies change, even revolution.'

'Are there any other perspectives on transformational leadership that I need to be aware of?'

'Well, you could have a look at Kouzes and Posner. Their model is more prescriptive than the above in that they turn the descriptions of Burns, Bass, and Bennis and Nanus into five actions. So they say that the transformational leaders should model the way for their followers by acting as a role model and setting a personal example of how they expect their followers to act. Secondly, they should inspire their followers by producing a vision that people want to follow. Thirdly, they must challenge current processes and change the ways the organisation does things, and if this requires a change in the current status quo so be it. Fourthly, they must give subordinates the freedom to act autonomously and encourage them to do so within reasonable limits. And, finally, they should encourage and motivate staff by recognising and rewarding their achievements and hard work.' Martin paused and looked at me. 'You still don't look very enthusiastic about TL.'

'That's because, even if we leave aside my concerns for how transformational leadership can be corrupted by individuals, I find it hard to see how this approach can work in education where every teacher has their own vision of what education is,' I said.

'It's for this reason that Middlehurst suggests that transformational leadership may not be successful in universities and by extension other educational establishments because: (a) a dual authority exists, namely administrative and professional; (b) the teacher's loyalty is often to their discipline or the department rather than the institution and (c) teachers find motivation in the nature of the work they do and can often resist attempts at extrinsic motivation by leaders.'

'That's interesting, considering what we said earlier about TL being the dominant leadership theory in education. Does anyone else agree with Middlehurst's views?'

'Oh, yes. Hargreaves suggests that the most effective principal may not be the heroic visionary posited by transformational theory, but a pragmatist who steers the school through choppy waters and develops new aims and strategies as the external demands on the school change.'

'This could be seen as support for Middlehurst's view that transactional leadership may be more successful with teachers than transformational approaches'.

'That might well be the case. Anyway, let's leave it today. Here's a handout (page 139) summarising the strengths and weaknesses of charismatic and transformational leadership for you to peruse.'

'What are we looking at next week?' I asked.

'Distributed leadership, so have a read.'

Nat's reflection

7 November

Why am I so suspicious of charismatic and transformational leadership? The question is still bugging me. This requires a cup of tea and a think.

OK, I don't like transformational leadership because:

- It places too much emphasis on the leader and makes them out to be almost superhuman. I don't like or trust that sort of hero worship.

- To be a transformational leader, you must be driven by a set of values. Actually working out what your values are, what principles you are willing to 'die' for is a very difficult and time-consuming task. Very few busy managers/leaders ever do this. Therefore, their vision may be built upon the clay of expediency rather than the rock of genuine values and principles. So why should I sign up to them?

- In education, transformational leadership is based on a falsehood, i.e. that every principal in the country can have a vision for their school or college. But their vision will have to be in line with what the Department for Education and OfSTED want. Otherwise they will face considerable difficulties. So they have to compromise and their vision becomes the government's, with just some minor variations at the margin.

- Transformational leadership seems to give all the credit for improvements in the school to the principal. How often do we see the headline 'Superhead saves failing school'? This ignores the fact that if a school is failing, it receives additional funding/support from the Department for Education, OfSTED and the local authority. There is also an influx of new staff; poorly performing staff are encouraged to leave and the old staff that remain roll up their sleeves in an effort to prove that they are not poor teachers. Even learners can react against the negative criticism by declaring, 'We'll show them just how good we can be'.

- As a theory, it promotes an anti-democratic way of dealing with staff and contains elements of manipulation.

Reading the above, I sound like the radical student who was asked, 'What are you campaigning against?' and replied, 'What have you got?' There are clearly aspects of transformational leadership that are valuable – such as creating a personal connection with each follower. I'll need to think about which aspects I can integrate into my leadership style.

Space for your notes

Prompts

- Have you ever worked for a leader who had a clear vision for the school/ college? How did you feel about their leadership style?
- Besides the principal, who is essential to the success of your school or college?

Record of tutorial

Summary notes from tutorial held on 3 November

- Weber described charisma as a special personality characteristic which few people possess. In reality, charisma may be a complex mixture of several qualities, such as self-confidence, good communication skills, sociability and the power to dominate groups.

- Charismatic leaders expect followers to demonstrate unquestioning trust, loyalty and respect. This means that followers are required to adopt the leader's ideology, beliefs and values as their own and demonstrate affection and concern for the leader.

- The very nature of charismatic leadership means that it can be used to manipulate the followers for the leader's own personal gain.

- However, charismatic leadership as a theory and practice is not inherently unethical. It is therefore important to separate the theory from the unscrupulous actions of leaders.

- It is entirely possible to be a charismatic leader without being a transformational leader.

- Transformational leaders appeal to the better natures/higher order values and morals of their followers. They ask their followers to transcend their own self-interest for the good of the group or organisation. In aligning themselves with a greater cause, followers can grow, develop and (perhaps) self-actualise as individuals.

- Not all transformational leaders are highly charismatic but all will have an element of charisma.

- Burns saw transformational leadership as residing on the same continuum as transactional leadership. He believed that most transactions between leader and follower were of a transactional kind. However, whenever transformational transactions occur, the motivation and moral intentions of both parties are raised above that of self-interest.

- Central to transformational leadership is the leader's attention to the needs of the follower (contrast this with the charismatic leader's relationship with followers). Once the follower's needs are identified, the leader seeks to show how these can be achieved by alignment with the group's or organisation's goals.

- Transformational leaders ask followers to transcend their own interests for those of the group or organisation. The reward for this sacrifice is belonging to something that is bigger than the individual.

- People who use transformational leadership for their own selfish purposes and in unethical ways are, according to Bass and Riggio, pseudo-transformational leaders because they have no concern for the needs of their followers.

- Bass identified four Is as the essential components of TL.

- First: Individualised influence (charisma). The leader draws people to him/her and models the behaviour that they expect followers to adopt. This attraction and modelling leads to the followers' accepting the leader's vision for the organisation as their own.

- Second: Inspirational motivation. The leader expects people to excel. This unconditional belief in their abilities inspires and motivates the followers and their performance improves. This creates a virtuous circle of continuous improvement and personal growth is created. This improvement in self-image and well-being creates in the followers feelings of gratitude, and an emotional link is created with the leader.

- Third: Intellectual stimulation. Followers are encouraged to question current practices and to seek new and improved ways of operating. They are also encouraged to question their own values and beliefs and to examine attitudes (often formed in childhood – such as believing the teacher who told them that they would never amount to anything) that might be holding them back.

- Fourth: Individualised consideration. The transformational leader seeks to form a one-to-one relationship with followers. The leader is happy to listen to followers' suggestions and ideas and provides them with opportunities to grow and develop as employees and individuals.
- Bennis and Nanus suggest that transformational leaders share four attributes.
- First, they have a clear vision for the organisation which is realistic and achievable.
- Secondly, they seek to shape organisational culture and support shared values as a means of achieving congruence of aims between leader and followers. Such agreement improves the chances of achieving the leader's objectives.
- Thirdly, they demonstrate through words and deeds where they stand on issues and are consistent and predictable in their behaviour (according to Goleman, staff trust leaders who are predictable).
- Fourthly, transformational leaders have a clear and accurate view of their strengths and weaknesses. They do not suffer from false modesty, nor do they delude themselves about what they can and can't do well.
- Tichy and De Vanna see transformational leaders as change agents. The leader's vision provides the required road map for organisational change. Not only do transformational leaders seek to break down old structures and practices but they also encourage their followers to do the same. The change process offers opportunities to both the leader and followers for personal growth and development.
- Kouzes and Posner turn the broadly descriptive theory of transformational leadership into a prescriptive theory by suggesting that transformational leaders should:
  - first, model the way they want followers to act
  - secondly, inspire and spread their vision for the future of the organisation
  - thirdly, challenge current practices and procedures and encourage followers to do the same
  - fourthly, enable others to act independently
  - fifthly, encourage and motivate others by rewarding good work (note the reward need not be monetary).

- Despite transformational leadership becoming the 'theory of choice' in education, Middlehurst is concerned that it may be inappropriate in educational organisations, as academics are often wedded to their discipline or department and, as professionals concerned with the well-being of their learners, their motivation is intrinsically generated.

- Middlehurst was concerned that teachers may resent the application of external motivation and see it as manipulation. For these reasons, she believed that transactional leadership was more appropriate in universities and, by extension, other educational establishments.

- Hargreaves argues that the successful principal may not be the visionary described by transformational leadership theory, but rather a pragmatist that navigates through difficult waters.

Implications of learning for my leadership style

Although I have a few principles, I am at heart a pragmatist. But transformational leadership is the theory of choice in education today. If I wish to reach the top, I have to at least demonstrate aspects of the approach in how I manage and lead people. So what can I do?

First, I need a generic vision for education that I can use as a starting point for each job I apply for. I will then need to amend my template to reflect the nature and current needs of each organisation that I apply to. My vision must be based upon my education philosophy and what I think are the aims and purposes of education; otherwise, I'm just being another hypocritical con man who can spin a good line. That might get me a job but it wouldn't take staff too long to see through me. It won't be easy to sort out exactly what I believe about education and condense it into a few key phrases, but it's well worth doing. Even if I never apply for another job again, I will have made explicit what I stand for. That's valuable in its own right because if 'you don't know what you stand for, you will stand for anything'. Education leaders need a set of principles to guide their decision making. I need a set of principles.

Secondly, I do like the idea of creating a connection with every follower and listening to what they have to say. At times, when I'm under pressure, I often cut this process short. I need to be on my guard against this.

Thirdly, I should encourage staff to try out new ideas and processes. But, being cautious, I'll need to establish the parameters within which staff can act. If they want to go beyond the set boundaries, they will have to talk to me. I need some general ground rules for this.

Fourthly, I need to give more recognition to the achievement and work of staff. Even if it's a simple 'Thank you' or 'Well done'. Staff need to be valued and made to feel appreciated and I don't do enough of that.

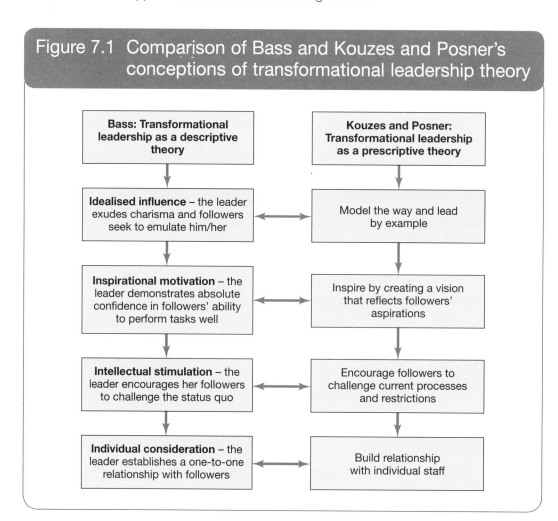

Figure 7.1 Comparison of Bass and Kouzes and Posner's conceptions of transformational leadership theory

Handout

Table 7.1 Strengths and weaknesses of charismatic leadership

Strengths
Although the term 'charismatic leader' is difficult to define, there are numerous examples of such leaders in both fiction and reality. If anything, it is the fictitious and idealised versions of historical characters that influence people's perceptions of, and desire for, such leaders the most.
The theory has an intuitive appeal. Followers want their leader to be special.
There are people who possess an almost magical ability to draw people to them.
Followers can develop a fierce loyalty towards their leader.
Confidence/blind faith in the leader can enable the followers to achieve astonishing results.
Followers often feel that they have been chosen or are especially fortunate to find such a leader.

Weaknesses
It lacks conceptual clarity and says nothing about how charismatic leaders should act.
Charisma is seen as a character trait rather than a learned behaviour, which reinforces the view that only 'certain people are born to lead', which leads us back to the discredited 'great man' theory of leadership.
If charisma is an inherent trait, then it is not possible to teach it to prospective leaders.
Charismatic leadership is elitist and anti-democratic.
Descriptions of charismatic leaders are often only applicable to the principal of an organisation and not leaders at lower levels.
In the wrong hands, charismatic leadership can be abused to the detriment of followers on a grand scale, e.g. Hitler, Jim Jones (Google the James Town massacre), David Korresh (Google the Wako, Texas massacre).
Charismatic leadership does not provide any guidance on how leaders should act.

Table 7.2 Strengths and weaknesses of transformational leadership

Strengths
It has been widely researched.
Has an intuitive appeal – vision of the leader leading by example from the front.
The needs of the followers are important to the leader.
Provides a broad view of leadership that augments other leadership models.
Places strong emphasis on values, ethics and morals. Note that supporters claim that this emphasis on morality means that Hitler, Stalin, Jim Jones et al. are not true leaders – this view can be contested.

Weaknesses
It lacks conceptual clarity: because it covers so many functions and roles, it is difficult to define the parameters of transformational leadership.
Transactional and transformational leadership can be seen too simplistically as a choice between two opposite approaches when they should be seen as two approaches that can be combined.
Transformational leadership can be seen as a character trait rather then a learned behaviour, which leads us back to the notion 'certain people are born to lead' and /or versions of the 'great man' theories.
Transformational leadership can appear elitist and/or anti-democratic.
Descriptions of transformational leadership often imply that the theory can only be applied by the principal of an organisation and not leaders at lower levels.
As with charismatic leadership, transformational leadership has the potential to be abused. (The idea that corrupt leaders are pseudo-transformational leadership can be challenged on the grounds that they use exactly the same tools as ethical leaders to achieve their aims and objectives.)
Transformational leadership does not provide a clearly defined set of assumptions about how leaders should act in particular situations; rather, it provides a general way of thinking about leadership that emphasises ideals, inspiration, innovation and ethics.

Additional information on the issues covered by this tutorial can be found at/in:

- www.pearsoned.com/mcgrathandcoles
- www.businessballs.com
- **Bass, B.M.** (1985) *Leadership and Performance Beyond Expectations*. New York: Free Press.
- **Bennis, W. and Nanus, B.** (1985) *Leaders: The Strategies for Taking Charge*. New York: Harper Row.
- **Northhouse, P.G.** (2007) *Leadership Theory and Practice*, 4th edn. London: Sage.

Management gurus and the birth of distributed leadership

Aim of the tutorial

By the end of the tutorial you will be able to briefly outline the management and leadership theories of three major management gurus and explain how distribution leadership is a rejection of the great man theory of leadership.

Contents

- The advent of management gurus: Drucker, Peters and Covey
- Emphasis on the single heroic leader model of leadership since the 1980s
- Distributed leadership a rejection of the leader as hero
- Definitions of distributed leadership
- Competing versions of distributed leadership
- A typology of distributed leadership

Nat's reflection

10 November

Well, we've almost covered all the leadership theories. Today Martin wants to look at distributed leadership. I'm not at all sure that there is such a theory. It seems to be another one of those cases where an academic, looking to make a name for themselves, has taken an existing notion, in this case delegation, given it a new name and claimed that they've developed a new theory.

I seem to be in a cynical phase – first I had a downer on LMX charismatic and transformational leadership and now it's distributed leadership's turn. It's a good thing to be critical of theories and what people write, but I need to avoid becoming cynical. I should give new ideas a fair hearing before I reject them. So I'll be positive and listen to what Martin has to say.

Review of tutorial

Martin was with another student when I arrived and I spent five minutes waiting while he finished up. It gave me a chance to have a look at the notice boards. There were a number of conferences advertised by various academic and professional societies. It suddenly struck me that other than belonging to a teachers' union I belonged to no professional organisations. As someone interested in education management and leadership, I should give some serious consideration to joining **BELMAS**, The British Education Leadership and Administration Society. The fees didn't look too bad and the annual conference was at Oxford, so I could indulge my *Morse* fantasies.

Finally Martin's door opened and he ushered the student out. '**Sorry to keep you,**' he said. '**The deadline for the first MA assignments is fast approaching and students are panicking. How are things? Have you got over your suspicions of charismatic and transformational leadership yet?**'

'Only partly.'

'Well, before we look at distributed leadership, I thought I might feed your paranoia a bit more by very briefly looking at the thoughts of three well-known management gurus.'

'Wonderful,' I sighed in mock exasperation.

'Well, the first one is not really a guru: he's probably the only real genius that management studies has ever thrown up. He's Peter Drucker. He was born in 1909 and died in 2005. His most famous books were probably *The Practice of Management*, and *Management: Tasks, Responsibilities and Practices*. But the one I suggest you get hold of is the *Essential Drucker* which was published in 2007. It's a really good summary of his ideas. He believed that the only purpose of a business was to create and keep a customer and that everything else – profits, growth, reputation – grew from that. If you can remember back to our third tutorial you used his definition of management to describe what a manager does.'

'Oh yeah. It was to set objectives, organise, motivate and communicate with staff and measure performance and develop people including ourselves.'

'You do remember. Well, we don't want to go over old ground. But just think about what he said about creating a customer. I don't like to call learners or students customers; to my mind, that devalues the relationship that exists between the teacher and learner. But Drucker's central point is that the customer/student/learner should be at the centre of everything we do. Every decision we make should be aimed at improving the service we give our students. Unfortunately, far too often decisions made in universities, colleges and schools are for the benefit or convenience of staff or management. We need to redress that.'

'I agree, but very often managers and staff think that what's good for them is good for the students.'

'So challenge it. In later life Drucker suggested that when things were stable and there were no threats on the horizon managers should concentrate on improving how to do day-to-day activities, but in periods of change they needed to be more creative and identify new opportunities and new ways of doing things. Effectively, he championed the idea that managers always had to be proactive...'

'And, if you are constantly proactive, that gives you the opportunity to challenge existing processes and procedures for the benefit of learners.'

'Exactly. Now, as I say, Drucker was not known for the development of any specific theory. He was instead a commentator on modern management practices. His great talent was his ability to identify trends before they were recognised by others. Trends that other, less gifted, thinkers picked up and ran with, often making a fortune in the process. So, for example, in *The Age of Discontinuity* he identified that change management was likely to become increasingly important over the years. This, when many companies had huge corporate planning teams developing strategic plans for the next 5, 10 and even 20 years.'

'I always wondered why strategic management died a death in the 80s.'

'It was the first oil crisis in the early 1970s that woke people up to the fact that you couldn't plan for the future based upon extrapolating what had happened previously. Change is discontinuous. This insight caused cracks to appear in the corporate planning edifice, and these were widened by the industrial unrest that was so much a feature of the 70s and early 80s. And the final nail in the coffin was the information technology revolution. After that, it was obvious that planning had to be non-linear and take account of unexpected changes in the business environment. I mean, who in the 80s would ever have envisaged the impact that the internet would eventually have on how we do business and education?'

'But we still do plenty of planning, don't we?'

'Indeed we do. But we now do it on the basis of uncertainty and usually over a much smaller timescale. It was Drucker who predicted what is now called the age of post-industrialism and examined the impact that this would have on management practices. He was among the first to argue for the end of hierarchical organisational structures and the introduction of leaner, flatter structures.'

'So someone still worth reading?'

'Most definitely. In the 80s Tom Peters came to the fore with two huge best selling books: *In Search of Excellence* with Robert Waterman and *A Passion for Excellence* with Nancy Austin. Peters was the quintessential management guru. His seminars were entertainment events, his delivery was humorous, powerful and full of energy. He had a number of themes which he promoted and these included the need for managers to develop and communicate a vision for the organisation.'

'As in transformational leadership?' I asked.

'Yes. He also advocated that managers, staff and organisations should develop values and act with integrity, which again has obvious links to transformational leadership theory. In addition, he wanted organisations to promote innovation and recognise that good ideas often come from the staff at the bottom of the organisation rather than the top. He labelled such valuable staff as 'skunks' because often they had to work in the shadows, act almost as guerrilla fighters, and overcome significant resistance to get their ideas accepted. Why do you think that good ideas come from the bottom rather than the top?'

The question was unexpected and took me by surprise. Finally, I composed a half-decent answer. 'The people at the bottom are the ones that are in touch with the customer: they know what the customer wants and this enables them to respond quickly to change.'

'Exactly. You don't need market research to find out what your customers want if you communicate with front line staff daily. That's why education leaders should spend more time listening to teachers and teaching assistants rather than the latest bright idea from a think tank whose members probably went to the best possible schools in their area and from there to Oxbridge. In order for staff to respond to the customers' wants, Peters argued that organisations should control staff using a loose–tight approach.'

'You mean, like one of those dog leads that allow the dog to run up to 25 metres but which you can snap closed at any time?' I suggested.

'Exactly. Give staff a clearly defined area of action in which they can exercise their discretion, but if they wish to go beyond that they need to seek permission. He was also a great advocate of organisations sticking to what they know best and not trying to get involved in stuff that they know nothing about.'

'So he wouldn't be a fan of free schools then?'

'Being a believer in free markets, he probably would support free schools. But he would argue that principals needed to employ financial experts to manage the funding, leaving them free to manage the staff and promote their vision for education. He also saw the value of symbols, stories and heroes for organisations. He believed that the organisation's culture could be both a unifying and motivational factor.'

'So who's your last guru?'

'Stephen Covey and his *Seven Habits of Highly Effective People®*.'

'I went on a course run by the Covey Foundation back in the 90s on the Seven Habits.'

'So you can tell me about them.'

Will I never learn to keep my mouth shut? I collected my thoughts and started to reel off what I could remember. 'First, be proactive. Don't sit about waiting for something to happen: try to anticipate events. That way, you can exercise some control over your own environment rather than be controlled by events. Secondly, begin with the end in mind, meaning that you should have a picture in your mind of what outcome you want even before you start. So don't start to design a computer system for the school unless you know what you want it to do. You should then work on those activities that will help you achieve your objectives and avoid distractions. Thirdly, put first things first, meaning prioritise tasks according to importance not urgency. What's important are those tasks that will help us achieve our objectives as established in habit 2.'

'That's a good point. Too often we react to the urgent telephone call and leave the important task that we're doing.' Martin said.

'Fourthly, think win-win. Don't look to defeat people in an argument or gain an advantage; instead, think of ways in which both parties can benefit fairly from any decision. This approach will often lead to future joint activities. Fifthly, seek first to understand, then be understood, which basically means that you should listen to the other person and understand where they are coming from before you try to explain your position or offer an opinion on what they should do.

'It's the old doctor's maxim dressed up for business: "always diagnose before you prescribe".' Martin said.

Sixthly, synergise, which is about working with others because two people working together will produce more than the combined output of two people working separately. And, finally, sharpen the saw, which is really an injunction to take time out for your own mental, physical, emotional and intellectual needs; otherwise, you will become rusty and perform badly.'

'Very good. If you want to read more about Gurus then you can search on Google. But for now, let's turn to distributed leadership.'

'Before we do that, can you answer one question for me? Why did Peters, Covey and the other gurus became so popular in the 1980s?'

'It could be a variety of reasons. With Margaret Thatcher and Ronald Reagan in power, capitalism became fashionable and suddenly being an entrepreneur or manager was sexy. Don't forget that this was the time of the "yuppies" and the first *Wall Street* film. But it might also have something to do with a book that was published in the 1970s which sold millions around the world called *Up the Organisation* by Robert Townsend. He'd been Chairman of Avis Rent-a-Car Corporation in the States and he wrote a book that was quirky, funny and full of excellent advice and ideas for managers. After his mega success,

publishers were looking for the next big thing in popular management books and this brought about the birth of the management guru.'

'So there was a bandwagon effect.'

'I think that was part of it.'

Nat's reflection

11 November

There are so many 'airport' books on management and leadership these days. Countless trees must have died in their production. And they all promise to show you the one true way to be a great leader. If only it were that simple.

I've read quite a few of them. My favourite title was 'The Leadership Secrets of Attila the Hun'. Unfortunately we're not allowed to use his methods for dealing with underperforming staff. I usually find something in each book of interest, but you can't manage according to a recipe given in some book. It's more complicated than that. You have to take into account context and organisational culture. I mean, the situation in a top American company and a British school is very different. What works in one can't be applied in its entirety in the other. But that doesn't mean that you can't transfer some of the ideas. The trick is identifying the usable bits.

Of all of the gurus mentioned I think I can learn most from Drucker. I've read him before, and I know from a quick Amazon search that there is a new book out called 'The Essential Drucker'. I'll get it and have a read. It won't be specific to education but if, as Martin says, Drucker deals in principles, then many of those principles should apply to any situation where a leader or manager is trying to influence staff. I could probably learn a lot by looking at other sectors — provided I don't fall into the trap of believing that I can just import ideas willy-nilly and expect them to work.

Space for your notes

Prompts

- Which popular management books have you read/looked at?
- Which did you like best? Why?
- What ideas could you use at work?

Review of tutorial

'So, distributed leadership. What is it and how did it start?' I asked, so preventing Martin from asking me what I knew about distributed leadership. Which in truth was not much.

'Perhaps because the 80s was the age of individualism, many of the management books written at that time dealt with the heroic leader saving her company from ruin by the force of her personality and the use of a magic leadership theory which any reader could learn for the price of the book. The result has been that, since the 1980s, policy makers have placed great emphasis on the need for a strong leadership. Therefore, it's hardly surprising that the model of leadership that has been promoted by various governments emphasises the role of the individual leader. This led to the return of the "great man theory" of leadership. But by the 1990s Harris and others came to believe that this emphasis on one gifted individual who has all the skills required to run a successful school had severe limitations and did not reflect the reality of school leadership.'

'Well, despite what they say, the idea that leadership should reside in the hands of a single person, or very small group of people, within an organisation is still the model I work with every day,' I said. 'And it annoys me that these "gifted leaders" are described as visionary, charismatic or transformational and are perceived as more important to organisational success than mere followers or managers. It's as if the rest of us play no part in school success.'

'Gronn would agree with you. In 2003 he said that "Such Exceptionalism … represents the triumph of super-leadership". In particular, he's critical of the leader–follower binary that underpins much of orthodox leadership studies, as it implies that the leader has all the influence and ideas while the followers exercise little influence and are largely powerless. Like you, he thinks that it is very rare for an organisation to have only one leader. He argues that, dependent on time, place and circumstances, organisations have many leaders acting within their own sphere of influence. He argues that the emphasis on a single leader obscures the actual relationships that exist in the workplace and is therefore unhelpful because it doesn't represent the reality of leadership in schools and colleges.'

'I agree,' I said.

'Other commentators like Middlehurst, Ogawa and Bossert, and Fidler have all argued that although leadership from a senior figure is important it can also be provided by others in the organisation. They view leadership as a collective practice which flows through the many roles and networks that exist in any organisation. Indeed, they argue that the very complexity of modern educational institutions makes it essential that more than one person be involved in the process.'

'What you describe seems to be a lot of people trying to define a concept that defies definition,' I said.

'I have to admit that as yet there is no agreed definition of distributed leadership. However, Bennett et al. suggest that it contains three distinctive elements. First, it exists within any group of individuals that are working together. This is a very different notion from the idea that leadership emanates only from the anointed leader. Secondly, distributed leadership increases the number of people who can be involved in leadership. It is no longer only open to the few but becomes available to the many. Thirdly, distributed leadership recognises that knowledge and expertise are widely distributed in organisations and that to maximise performance it is necessary to access these multiple sources.'

'I'm not sure that that makes it any clearer,' I said.

'Perhaps not, but the above definition has parallels with Harris's suggestion that distributed leadership implies that there are multiple sources of expertise, guidance and direction available to staff within any organisation, and that what stops these multiple sources causing chaos is that they all share and understand the organisation's common culture.'

'So it's a case of the organisation's culture providing the tight/loose control within which these multiple leaders operate? I asked.

'**That and the principal,**' Martin said.

'So what's the role of delegation in all of this?'

'Mere delegation is not synonymous with distributed leadership as delegation implies continued dependency and accountability. Genuine distributed leadership requires those in leadership positions to relinquish some power to others. The relationship between leaders and followers then becomes one of interdependency rather then dependency. The relationship is less hierarchical than in cases where an all-powerful figure delegates work to a subordinate.'

'I'm sympathetic to the spirit of distributed leadership. I mean, it's obvious that everyone contributes and leads at different times. But the theory as you've outlined sounds like a recipe for confusion, with multiple leaders and no one in charge.'

'In which case I've obviously not explained it very well. Distributed leadership does not mean that everyone leads. If that were the case, leadership as an activity would cease to be distinctive. There is, and will always remain, a need for someone to retain overall responsibility for the organisation. Indeed, this may be essential to satisfy the demand for accountability from the organisation's many stakeholders. Instead, it should be thought of as the sharing of leadership among formal and informal leaders over time. At the heart of distributed leadership reside collaboration, mutual trust, support and a willingness to share power. The purpose of distributed leadership is to maximise human performance within the organisation.'

'So how do you avoid confusion as to roles and responsibilities?'

'Well, Harris suggests that to avoid confusion and create an environment in which distributed leadership can flourish it is essential to first establish clear ground rules that formally appointed leaders such as the principal and deputies have to follow. Secondly, describe how formal leaders share responsibility for leadership with informal leaders. This process identifies what functions and responsibilities will remain with those holding formal leadership positions. Thirdly, identify the boundaries within which informal leaders can exercise leadership. Clearly, this approach retains a certain allegiance to hierarchical power, i.e. those at the top set the ground rules. But even so, it requires the principal to redistribute power within the organisation by giving to those who do not occupy formal leadership positions responsibility for important areas of work.'

'I'm not convinced that such delegation can lead to distributed leadership; after all, the power still resides with the person doing the delegation.'

'Well, maybe you'd prefer Gronn's version, rather than Harris's delegated process; he sees distributed leadership as a spontaneous collaboration between members of staff that results in distributed practice: for example, when two or more members of staff exercise their own discretion to work together on an issue of mutual interest and rely on each other for support and direction rather than management.'

'But Gronn's version sounds like something that teachers have been doing for years, i.e. working in partnership with colleagues. Therefore, in assigning the term "distributed leadership" to such practices, he's simply recognising something that has always existed in well-run organisations, namely the willingness of individuals to take responsibility.'

'You might well be right. But it is still valuable to identify and describe such practices, as it helps us to analyse and understand the complex relationships that exist in the workplace. Here, I've written a typology of the different distributed leadership models that might exist in a school or college. I'm sure that others could be added. Have a look at it when you look at the strengths and weaknesses of the distributed leadership (see Tables 8.1 and 8.2).'

'OK', I said.

'Next time we'll look at the leader's role in change management', Martin said and started to stand up.

Nat's reflection

13 November

What do I think of distributed leadership? What is it exactly? Is it a non-theory?

I fully accept that there is something in the notion of distributed leadership because I see it in operation every day of the week. But I've always called that 'something' team work or collegiality. Is it really a separate form of leadership? Getting a handle on this is really hard.

If I have to pick one definition, I think I prefer Gronn's idea of spontaneous working together. But I don't have to get too hung up on trying to define it and distinguish it from other types of behaviour; I just need to create the environment in which it can flourish. Because, clearly, it is beneficial to the organisation. The more people I can encourage to take responsibility and act proactively within the school, the better.

I read years ago that, when Ford were launching the Mondeo on to the market, senior management were tied up with something else and left it to the middle managers to promote the car. The result was the most successful launch of a new car in Ford's history. From that start, the Mondeo has gone on to be one of Ford's best-selling cars ever.

Ford's experience just goes to show that if you leave good people alone to get on with their job they usually do a good job. It's unnecessary interference that causes problems. After all, if you don't trust people and give them a chance to show what they can do, how can they ever develop?

Space for your notes

Prompts

- Are there any examples of distributed leadership in your school or college?
- If there are, which model of distributed leadership do they most resemble: Harris's delegated model or Gronn's spontaneous model?

Record of tutorial

Summary notes from tutorial held on 10 November

- Peter Drucker (1909–2005) believed that the sole purpose of any business was to create a customer and maintain a good relationship with them. Schools should try to do the same with learners, parents and other stakeholders.
- To enable businesses to fulfil their purpose, Drucker suggested that managers should be concerned with five functions. These are: setting objectives, organising staff, motivating and communicating with staff, measuring performance and developing people, including themselves.
- Every decision we take as education leaders should be aimed at improving the service we provide to learners.
- Drucker suggests that in periods of stability managers should seek to improve the way they do things, but in periods of rapid change they should look at doing new things in order to survive.

- Drucker did not promote a particular theory of management or leadership; instead, he identified trends which later writers developed. For example, in the late 60s he wrote about the need for change management as a discrete activity and the need for leaner less hierarchical organisations. Both trends only entered the mainstream management thinking in the late 70s/80s.

- Tom Peters wrote of the need for managers to: create a vision for their staff to follow, develop a set of shared values with the help of staff, promote innovation, recognise that good ideas often came from the bottom where staff are talking to customers, stick to what the organisation knows best, exercise a tight/loose control over the staff and shape the organisational culture to support the vision and attitudes that leaders want to develop.

- Stephen Covey's Seven Habits of Highly Effective People® are: be proactive, begin with the end in mind, put first things first, think win–win, seek first to understand and only then to be understood, synergise and sharpen the saw.

- Management gurus came to the fore in the 1980s when the success of capitalism and the new neo-liberal philosophy of the right was popularised by Mrs Thatcher in Great Britain and President Reagan in the United States of America. At the same time, publishers responded to the glorification of managers as the new heroes by promoting popular management texts as never before.

- The glorification of managers led to a resurgence of the great man theory of leadership. Once more, leaders were seen as exceptional individuals with extraordinary powers that only a few possessed.

- The view of heroic leaders capable of transforming failing organisations was adopted by the public sector, including education, as the model of leadership that was desirable.

- Gronn dislikes such exceptionalism as it diminishes the role that others play in the success of schools.

- Proponents of distributed leadership accept that it is important to have a senior leader who represents the school to the outside world and is ultimately responsible, but they also believe that there is room for other leaders.

- Bennett et al. describe distributed leadership as a phenomenon that: first, exists within any group of individuals that are working together; secondly, that increases the number of people who can be involved in leadership, meaning that leadership is no longer only open to the few but becomes available to the many; thirdly, recognises that knowledge and expertise are widely distributed in all organisations.

- Mere delegation is not distributed leadership as it implies continued dependency on a higher authority and places constraints on the actions of individuals. Genuine dispersed leadership involves giving power to others. The relationship between 'official leader' and 'unofficial leader' then becomes one of interdependence, not dependency.
- Distributed leadership does not mean that everyone leads. Someone has to maintain overall responsibility for the organisation.
- Distributed leadership involves sharing leadership between the many, not the few, and among the informal, not just the formal. It is this that marks it out as a separate theory.
- To avoid confusion over roles and responsibilities, Harris argues that clear ground rules have to be established in advance which stipulate and identify what responsibilities will remain the preserve of the formal leaders and identify the limitations of informal leaders' range of actions.
- Gronn does not see distributed leadership as an organised activity, rather as a process that arises naturally and spontaneously as a consequence of working in partnership/cooperation with colleagues.
- Gronn's version of distributed leadership may just describe an activity that has always existed in good organisations – namely, staff taking responsibility for functions without the involvement of formal leaders.

Implications of learning for my leadership style

Distributed leadership, or something very like it, happens in every school and college in the country. It's a fact of life. Therefore, I need to think about how best I can both encourage and utilise it. People aren't stupid. It's not true that if you give them an inch they'll pinch a mile. Well maybe the odd one will; but should I refuse to use a good idea simply because I'm afraid of a few taking advantage and causing problems? Of course not. Most people are cautious. They know the boundaries beyond which they should not go. So I'll commit myself to using distributed leadership.

But how do I get it off the ground? Certainly not by calling everyone together and telling them about this marvellous new leadership theory. No, I need to demonstrate through my actions that I want people to take on tasks and run with them with minimal interference from me. At the same time, I need to make it clear that if they run into problems they can come to me for advice, help and support. What I can't do is jump all over them if they fail or get it wrong. I have to be willing to accept honest mistakes.

Using distributed leadership requires me to trust people and allow them to do things their way. Provided they achieve the results required, I need to avoid the temptation to tell them how I'd do it. That's going to be tough for me. But I have to try. After all, twenty leaders in a school has to be better than one or two.

Figure 8.1 Envisaging the organisation structure where distributed leadership is practised

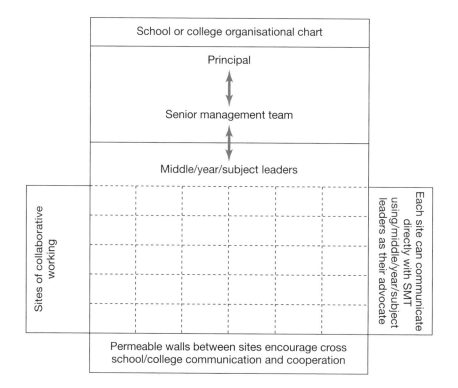

Handout

Table 8.1 A typology of distributed leadership

Typology	Occurs when the …
Dumped	Leader retains power and dumps responsibility on the individual without checking if they are willing and able to undertake the task and only intervenes when things go wrong.
Delegated	Leader retains ultimate power but checks if the person is willing and able to undertake the task and provides support when requested.
Divided	Leadership role is divided between two or more people who agree to share power.
Distributed	Leader empowers others to lead by encouraging collaboration and joint working. Power is redistributed to those who hold a formal or informal position in the organisation.
Democratic – within existing structures	Leader asks others for their opinions, and encourages collaboration and joint decision-making. Power is shared and everyone can participate, regardless of his or her position in the organisation.
Democratic – challenging existing structures	Individuals within an organisation challenge existing power structures, positions and practices and take power for themselves.
Dispersed	Organisation encourages the emergence of leaders in informal and spontaneous ways that may not be planned or approved of by the leader.

(Adapted from Rutherford, 2002)

Note: Within the dispersed category, it would be possible to subdivide it further according to the level of involvement and influence that the individual has in the decision-making process.

Table 8.2 The strengths and weaknesses of distributed leadership

Strengths
Distributed leadership is democratic and seeks to recognise that leadership can be exercised by the many not the few.
In today's complex world it is not reasonable to expect that a single person or small group of people can provide all the answers and exercise leadership throughout the organisation. Distributed leadership increases the number of leaders and spreads the burden of leadership.
Local knowledge available only to local leaders can improve the quality of decisions made within an organisation.
Distributed leadership provides opportunities for tomorrow's senior leaders to practise their skills.

Weaknesses
The theory remains underdefined and conceptually unclear.
Exactly how leadership and formal power is dispersed/delegated remains unclear.
Stakeholders want to have access to a single leader who retains accountability for the entire organisation.
Unless well coordinated, there is the danger that issues are not dealt with because of unclear lines of responsibility.

Additional information on the issues covered by this tutorial can be found at/in:

- www.pearsoned.com/mcgrathandcoles
- www.businessballs.com
- **Gronn, P.** (2002) 'Distributed leadership as a unit of analysis,' *The Leadership Quarterly* 13: 423–51.
- **Harris, A.** (2002) *Distributed Leadership in Schools: Leading or Misleading?* Paper presented at the British Educational Leadership and Management Association Annual Conference. Birmingham: University of Aston.

Leading change and motivating followers

Aim of tutorial

By the end of the tutorial you will be able to outline the stages that staff go through during a period of significant change and explain the key role that leaders play in the management of change.

Content

- Why the key function of any leader is to manage change
- Resistance to change
- Strategies for dealing with resistance to change
- Change agents
- Creativity and encouraging ideas from staff
- Stages in the change process
- Role of the leader in the change process
- The importance of communicating
- Maintaining staff motivation during periods of change

Nat's reflection

17 November

I can't believe that I have only one more session with Martin after today. I've really enjoyed our meetings and I've learnt more than I thought I would. I must remember to ask him to cover ethics in the final session.

But what exactly have I learnt? I suppose it's been the process more than anything. Martin hasn't tried to tell me how to lead. Instead he has relied on me to decide which theories or which parts of theories I want to build into my leadership style. This has worked well because I've had time between sessions to reflect on what we've discussed and for me to decide how the new learning fits into my leadership style.

But probably the single most important thing I've learnt is the partial nature of every theory. No single theory can fully describe what's going on, so you can't rely on just one theory as a leader. Like the good old days in Woolworths, you need to "Pick and Mix".

Anyway, today it's change management and motivation.

Review of tutorial

Martin looked up and smiled. On his desk was an array of sandwiches and Danish pastries. '**We had the MA Exam Board today and as always there was too much food. Here, help yourself,**' he said offering me a paper plate.

I selected a couple of sandwiches and a cake and sat down. 'It looks like Sarah Lund's going-away party' I said.

Martin's face lit up. '**You've been watching *The Killing?***' He asked.

'Of course. It's the *War and Peace* of crime drama.'

'**If you have time afterwards we can have a coffee and compare notes on who we think the killer is. Until then, let's talk about change management. I** assume that you are familiar with the better known motivational theories such as the **Hawthorne experiments**, **Maslow and Herzberg?**'

'I'm familiar with Maslow and Herzberg,' I replied.

'**Good. At the end of the session I just want to briefly discuss how they link into change theory.**'

'Fine,' I said, relieved not to be going over too much old ground.

'**Earlier in our discussions we agreed that the act of leading involved moving followers from point A to point B. Either in a physical or metaphorical sense.**' I nodded my head and Martin continued. '**There is a forward momentum in what leaders do, and it was this that distinguished them from managers who try to perfect the existing systems and processes without asking whether they are the right processes and practices. So leadership is about change, be that changing an organisation's culture or moving into new areas of work. As you are aware, not everyone is comfortable with change and most change is met with at least some resistance. How would you overcome such resistance?**'

I blew out my cheeks and started to outline the strategy I'd adopt. 'I think that most staff today recognise that change is here to stay. But we need to guard against complacency, so even if I was not planning a change I would try to create an organisational culture in which change was expected and seen by staff not as a threat but as a welcome challenge and opportunity. In that way I would be preparing them for any changes that might eventually come.'

'**Go on,**' Martin said.

'Communication is all important in any change situation. But, if there is little or no trust between the staff and management, it's very difficult to communicate with staff because they won't believe what you say. So leaders need to build trust by being fair, reasonable and open with staff over a period of time. Then when change does kick off, it is essential that staff are provided with accurate and up-to-date information about what is going on. Without it they will make up their own stories, and rumours will quickly circulate.' Martin nodded in agreement and I continued. 'It's also vital that staff are given adequate time to prepare for the change and that includes time to get used to the idea of change, time to discuss it, time to be trained for the change.'

'**Your last point is well made. Senior managers nearly always underestimate the time it takes to implement a major change. They seem to think that once they have made a decision it should be implemented overnight. Life's not like that,**' Martin said.

'I agree. From my experience what takes up the most time is dealing with the staff's feelings. A big change can be very emotional for staff. Leaders need to listen to staff, allow them to vent their feelings, frustrations and fears and give access to appropriate support if required.'

'**I agree,**' said Martin. '**This is precisely why good training is vital. Many people fear change because they have had a bad experience of it in the past. Therefore, along with training people in the new systems and processes, make sure that there are opportunities for staff to talk about their feelings and concerns.**'

'Training in the affective domain,' I said, remembering **Bloom's Taxonomy** of learning.

'**Exactly,**' said Martin. '**Staff are scared. They are afraid of the unknown. They aren't sure that they will be able to cope with the new procedures or systems, and when frightened people act irrationally.**'

'I know of at least a couple of very good people who, faced with the uncertainty of major change, resigned rather than face the pressure they felt they were under.'

'**When that happens it's down to poor leadership. As well as giving people a safe environment in which to express their concerns, leaders need to show confidence in their followers' ability. They can do this by celebrating and acknowledging the staff's existing skills and contribution to the organisation and expressing their confidence in the staff's ability to be equally successful in the new world. Anything else?**'

'I think staff have to be encouraged to become actively involved in the change process. The more involved they are with the process, the more they will own it. But management must listen to what they have to say as the work goes on.'

'**And how would you get staff involved?**' Martin asked.

'I'd try to identify individuals that have credibility with their colleagues, who could act as change agents or change champions. These people would be outside the normal management hierarchy…'

'**A case of distributed leadership?**' suggested Martin.

'I hadn't thought of it in those terms, but yes. I'd use these people to get the message out to staff and ask them to act as my eyes and ears on the ground so that I could nip any concerns in the bud before they could become a major problem.'

'**What else do you think helps minimise or deal with resistance?**' I sat and thought but nothing popped into my mind and Martin continued. '**There are some other simple things management can do. First, they need to demonstrate that the change has the full support of management, that there are no divisions. If there are any doubts or divisions among management, staff will pick up on this and seek to play one manager off against another in order to achieve their own aims. Secondly, leaders need to promote the benefits that the change will bring and demonstrate that there is minimal threat to the individual's autonomy, expertise and security.**'

'What do you mean by threat to the individual's autonomy?' I asked.

'**People take pride in their work. They like to believe that they have mastered it and are good at it and therefore don't have to be told how to do their job – they feel that they have a degree of autonomy.**'

'The freedom to do the job their way?'

'**Yes. They also like to think that, because they are good at their job and make a positive contribution to the organisation, they are valued and therefore safe from redundancy. The leader needs to reassure staff that if they engage fully with the training they will soon be making the same or an even greater contribution to the organisation.**'

'Which allays their fears?'

'**Yes. It's all part of the process of getting staff to accept the change project as their own. Leaders can do this by involving staff in the decision-making process from the start. This gives staff an opportunity to express their views, identify issues and suggest possible solutions. It is absolutely essential in times of change that management encourages as much communication as possible between staff and managers – upward, downward, sideways, diagonally. When it comes to lines of communication, every possible combination should be used. These channels allow leaders to understand and respond to the fears of staff. '**

Nat's reflection

18 November

I remember working in one college that was going through a period of rapid change. The senior management team called a meeting with all staff to talk about the change. They explained what was required and asked for suggestions as to how implementation should be handled. One brave soul said that the major problem in the college was a lack of two-way communication between the staff and SMT. The principal was appalled to hear this and said that he would form a committee for this very purpose which would meet bi-weekly with staff and continue in operation even after the change was completed. Staff thought this was an excellent idea and the meeting broke up in a very positive mood. Nothing more was ever heard about the committee again and the change was a near disaster! To paraphrase a once famous political jibe, 'That particular principal couldn't run a whelk stall, let alone a college'.

When I started working, emotions had to be left at home. People who showed emotions at work were considered untrustworthy. That view has changed, to some extent. But many managers and leaders are still surprised when people react emotionally to their carefully thought out strategy for changing the school. As a leader I'm aware of this, but I still don't always take full account of people's emotional investment in their job. I need to show more empathy. Put myself in the staff's shoes and try and work out how I'd feel if someone, whom I seldom see, came along and removed all the comfort and stability of the known for the supposed sake of improved efficiency.

Space for your notes

Prompts

- Have you ever been involved in a significant change at work? How did you feel about how the change was managed?
- Do you think that those feelings, positive or negative, have influenced your reaction to imposed change?

Review of tutorial

Taking a deep breath Martin said, '**OK, let's move on to the actual change process itself. There are a lot of different change process models and a number of them are a variation on the stages of bereavement. I've looked at a few and developed my own model which has seven stages. These are disbelief, bewilderment, resistance, searching for meaning, acceptance, internalisation and moving on.**'

'I think I see a book or article in your future,' I said with a laugh. 'But what do you mean by each of the terms?'

'**I thought you'd never ask. Here's a handout I prepared earlier,**' he said in his best *Blue Peter* voice (see handout on page 178 before reading on).

I read the handout out carefully and then said, 'It all looks very linear, as if one stage follows the other.'

'And you don't think it is linear?'

'No, I don't,' I said. 'If we're using the bereavement model, then, like getting over the death of a loved one, you don't move through it smoothly a stage at a time. One day you might reach the acceptance stage and then something happens, like a birthday or a song on the radio, to throw you back to the bewilderment and anger stage. I think you move up and down the scale several times before you actually reach internalisation and moving on. And like grief it's not something you can rush.'

'**I agree with you fully. I'd go so far as to say that it's more of a spiral than a straight line and you are able to move both up and down the spiral as the change progresses.** (See Figures 9.1 and 9.2, pages 176 and 177.) **However, once a person reaches the internalisation stage, it's extremely unlikely that they will slide back to an earlier state, but before that they could be moving up and down like a fiddler's elbow. Also, if it is a complicated change made up of several discrete changes, people will quickly accept certain aspects of the change and fully internalise them while still resisting other parts of the change.**'

'Let me get this right. Do you mean that the same person could be at different points on several different spirals?' I asked.

'**Yes. Now that level of complexity is really tough for a manager or leader to deal with and that's why communication is so important. But no one leader or manager can do all the communicating, so we are back to your idea of creating change agents or change champions: people in the organisation, at all levels, who are enthusiastic about the change but understand that not everyone feels the way they do. It's these people that leaders can use as conduits for communication with the staff. As they are generally closer to the staff than the leaders, they are better able to reassure and inform people on a daily basis.**'

'We've been talking about staff being resistant to change, but I've worked in places where it was the senior managers who resisted change. What do you make of that?' I asked.

'**It's a problem that is seldom addressed. I think that most SMTs have a sell-by date after which they need refreshing with new blood. Unfortunately, there are heads and principals out there who just want a quiet life and whose thinking is limited by today's patterns.**'

'Tell me about it. In one school I worked in, the principal said "Look, I've only got three years to go. When I'm gone you can make all the changes you like; until then, we do it the way we've always done it".'

'**What happened to her?**'

'There was an OfSTED inspection and she ended up retiring eighteen months early. But by then I'd left.'

'**That's the risk any principal runs if they don't adapt to changing requirements. It is precisely because older leaders can become set in their ways that they should encourage staff to be independent thinkers. Too often senior managers are suspicious of ideas from junior staff and find ways to discourage or block their initiatives.**'

'I've got to be honest, I don't get too many ideas from junior staff, even though I've made a point of inviting them to talk to me about their ideas.'

'**But have you created the right atmosphere in which creativity can flourish?**'

'How do you mean?'

'**Creativity and good ideas are generated when staff are relaxed, chatting informally and having a joke. Often someone makes an absurd or funny suggestion, but within it is the kernel of an idea that they or someone else is able to follow up and run with. Unfortunately, some leaders when they see staff shooting the breeze and having a laugh wrongly assume that they are just wasting time and jump on them.**'

'And so cut off the source of new ideas.'

'**Exactly. Along with inspiration and vision, good leaders need to provide space and opportunities for new ideas to flourish. That doesn't mean that they have to accept every crazy idea that crosses their desk. A valuable service that managers and leaders provide is to critically evaluate and amend the ideas put forward in order to make them workable.**'

'It sounds like you think that leaders should act as mentors for the leaders of tomorrow.'

'**Second only to leading change is the leader's responsibility to grow the leaders of tomorrow. Because if they don't, who will?**'

Nat's reflection

19 November

Martin's model of change isn't bad. But the stages aren't as discrete as the list implies. They overlap and elide into each other. Even so, I can recognise my own actions in several of the stages. There was a time in my early 30s when I lost my self-confidence and found it really tough to cope with change. I doubted my ability to adapt to the new technologies that were coming on stream. Of course I told no one and just kept a lid on it. It caused me a lot of stress. Daft really because, once the technology was installed and I was faced with a fait accompli, I just got on with it and learnt what I needed to know. Back to Knowles' **andragogy** and the idea that adults learn something when they have to and/or it's useful to them.

I hadn't really thought about the link between creativity and change before. But it's obvious really; new ideas create change. I need to think about how I can provide opportunities for staff to just 'shoot the breeze' as Martin described it. Ideas are created when people are relaxed and not afraid of suggesting something daft. From my own experience, there is nothing more certain to stifle ideas than to call a meeting to discuss the generation of new ideas. As if they can be summoned up on demand. Such meetings are made worse by the chair's contradictory claim that 'No idea is too silly to be considered', meaning that she expects people to make stupid suggestions. Perhaps I need to encourage staff to use the staffroom more and arrange a few low-key social events that would enable us to get together, have a chat and enjoy each other's company. Mind you, knowing my lot, it is just as likely to lead to a row as a new idea! But that's teachers for you, as rowdy as the kids — given half a chance. Hell, I do sound old and grumpy!

Space for your notes

Prompts

- Think of a major change that you have been involved in. How did it make you feel?
- On balance do you like or dislike change?
- What are the reasons for your like or dislike of change?

Review of tutorial

'OK, let's have a quick look at change and how you can use a few simple motivational ideas to help you through the process. What can you tell me about the Hawthorne experiments?'

'Not much. I've heard the term before but I've never read anything about them,' I said truthfully.

'Well, I think the Hawthorne experiments were one of the most interesting pieces of research ever done on management and motivation. It was carried out in the late 1920s and early 1930s at the Western Electric Hawthorne plant in Chicago. So it has nothing to do with West Bromwich Albion's football ground, as one undergraduate suggested to me! Basically, the researchers found that the working conditions for factory staff had very little impact on productivity, and that there was no correlation between increased production and improved working conditions. Instead, they found that the need to belong to a group and have status within it was more important than monetary incentives or good working conditions. In addition, they identified that informal groups of workers exercised a strong influence over the behaviour of workers.'

'So again it could be indicative of distributed leadership in action,' I said.

'Yes.'

'If that's the case, then management really needs to identify these informal groups and work through them,' I suggested.

'I agree. Managers and leaders need to be aware of these groups and the influence they exert. They can then create the conditions in which the groups can flourish and use them as a channel of communication during periods of change.'

'What else did the study identify?' I asked.

'They found that productivity went up as a result of the researchers and management talking to staff and involving them in decisions. Staff felt important and special. They responded positively to being treated with respect and asked for their opinions on issues that were normally the preserve of management. Remember, this was the late 1920s and early 1930s. Factory workers were viewed as an essential but easily replaceable resource, not as individuals that management entered into dialogue with.'

'Because there were millions unemployed during the Great Depression and staff were easily replaceable.'

'Correct. Unfortunately, the Hawthorne findings were shelved during the war and it wasn't until they were taken up by the Japanese and Volvo Cars in the 1960s/70s that they became widely understood and applied.'

'Interesting,' I said. 'I'll Google Hawthorne experiments and read up on it.'

'Do, but businessballs.com has a lot of good stuff on it, so start there. It was also just after the war that Maslow started his research on motivation and in 1954 he published his *Hierarchy of Needs*. (See Tutorial 6.) How do you think that his ideas link to change management?'

'Well people move up the hierarchy as their basic needs are met. If a significant change threatens the person's ability to meet their lower order needs for food, shelter, stable environment and freedom from threats, they are likely to become angry and afraid. And frightened people are unlikely to listen to what management say.'

'Precisely. But it's not just people's lower order needs that can be threatened by a big change. People's feeling of belonging, of being a valued member of a group and their need for the esteem of others can also come under threat. This can do serious harm to the person's self-respect and self-image.'

'So again the remedy for this is to reassure staff, keep them informed of what's going on and provide good training,' I said.

'I think you've got to go further than just keeping them informed. You need to engage them in a genuine two-way conversation and respond to what they say. People worry less if they think they have some influence over the events that are buffeting them.'

'So what about Herzberg's ideas on motivation? How do they fit into change management?', I asked.

'By telling us what factors do and don't motivate staff. Those factors that didn't motivate staff were what he called the hygiene factors or dissatisfiers and these included company policy, administration, supervision, level of salary, interpersonal relationships with supervisors, and working conditions. While the motivators were: the work itself, achievement, recognition, responsibility and advancement.'

'I know that he said that, no matter how good the hygiene factors were, they did not motivate staff; but if they were poor or below a reasonable standard, they demotivated staff.'

'Correct. His ideas owe something to the Hawthorne experiments. To motivate staff, he argued, leaders must recognise and celebrate the achievement of followers and provide staff with interesting and rewarding work. In addition, he thought that staff should be given responsibility and freedom to act within prescribed limits and provided with opportunities for advancement. You can see that all of these motivating factors have direct links to the work undertaken and little to do with the environment in which work is conducted.'

'So, when managing a change, we need to celebrate the various milestones that staff achieve on the way to completion of the entire task, give them a degree of freedom in which to manage the change for themselves and hold out the possibility of advancement after the change has been completed,' I said.

'Yep. That's about it. Now, how about that coffee and our chat about The Killing?'

'OK,' I said, 'but for our last session, can we look at ethics and leadership? It's not a topic that I know much about.'

'No problem. I'll dig something out. But for now who do you think the killer is?'

'My money is on the Mayor. Something fishy went on during the trip to Latvia.'

Nat's reflection

21 November

Other than the Hawthorne studies, I was familiar with the ideas on motivation that we discussed. But I have to say that I have failed to integrate the ideas around motivation into my management and leadership style. I tend to compartmentalise them and think about them as separate functions. It's as if I wake up and think, 'I need to motivate the staff today to do X'; the next day I think, 'Today I need to lead on this or that issue.' That's not an integrated strategy! I probably do it because I learnt each theory as a discrete idea and didn't spend enough time thinking about how they fitted together or how they were to be integrated into what I already knew.

It's not rocket science; change is about uncertainty and that causes anxiety. The best way to reassure and motivate staff is to talk to them. I remember one principal I worked with. She was seldom seen walking the corridors, and if she wanted to speak to you she summoned you to her office. After one particularly tough OfSTED inspection, she drew up an action plan which required significant reorganisation of the staff. The members of SMT did work with the staff to implement the change, but the principal's only contribution to the process was a series of emails addressed to individuals who had not achieved their change targets. Needless to say, her actions lost her a lot of credibility with the staff and caused much ill will.

Space for your notes

Prompts

- Is it possible to motivate another person?
- What motivates you?
- What demotivates you?
- What motivation strategies have you observed in your workplace and how successful have they been?

Record of tutorial

Summary notes from tutorial held on 17 November

- Leadership is concerned with movement. It's about moving followers forward. Therefore, it inevitably involves change. Leadership is concerned with initiating and managing change.
- Not everyone likes change and this can lead to resistance. To minimise resistance, leaders can:
  - instil in staff the acceptance that change is normal and should be seen as an opportunity rather than a threat
  - build trust with staff. Be frank and open with them. Say what they mean and mean what they say and be consistent in the message that they deliver
  - provide staff with accurate and up-to-date information on any proposed changes. Don't allow rumours to start
  - listen to the concerns of staff
  - allow staff sufficient time to prepare for the change and give them space to discuss the issues with colleagues
  - provide high-quality training.
- Many staff have had a bad experience of change. This can make them suspicious and resentful of change.

- The training provided has to recognise and deal with the staff's emotional responses to change.
- Leaders must create a safe environment in which people can air their views and feelings.
- To reassure staff, leaders should recognise the staff's previous achievements and express confidence in the staff's ability to be successful in the new environment.
- It's essential to get staff involved in the change process from the very earliest stages and allow them to influence the decision-making process.
- Early involvement ensures that staff buy into the change as something they helped to create.
- Leaders must establish multiple channels of communication with staff.
- Leaders should identify and use change agents/champions from among the staff ranks and use these people as communication conduits.
- To maximise the chances of a successful change, leaders should:
  - demonstrate that the entire management team supports the change
  - promote the benefits of the change to staff and the organisation
  - demonstrate that the change does not threaten the individual's autonomy, expertise or security of employment
  - encourage staff to buy into the change and see it as their own by involving them early in the change process
  - encourage as much open and frank communication between staff and management as possible.
- The stages in a major change can be likened to those of the mourning process. They are:
  - disbelief
  - bewilderment/anger
  - resistance
  - searching for meaning
  - acceptance
  - internalisation
  - moving on.
- The person does not progress through the stages in a smooth linear fashion. The process can be seen as circular, and events can push a person back to an earlier stage.

- Only when a person has reached the stage of internalisation is the danger of reverting to an earlier stage removed.

- In a big change, with many components, staff will be engaged in several change cycles and may be at a different stage on each of the cycles.

- The only way to deal with the complication posed by multiple cycles is to communicate with staff through change agents who work closely with the staff every day.

- It is not unknown for senior staff to resist change. If they cannot be won over to endorse the change, they should be removed for the good of the organisation.

- Seek new and creative ideas from junior staff by establishing the environment and opportunities in which creativity can flourish.

- Allow opportunities to socialise and 'shoot the breeze'.

- While leaders should encourage new ideas, they must also critically evaluate the ideas presented to them. Not every idea will be a winner.

- Leaders should mentor and develop the leaders of tomorrow.

- The Hawthorne experiments showed that:
  - working conditions have very little effect on productivity
  - belonging to a group and having status within that group is what matters to staff
  - informal work groups exercise great influence on the members' views
  - leaders must identify and work with these informal groups during periods of change
  - productivity went up at the Hawthorne plant because the researchers and managers showed an interest in the staff. Leaders should make followers feel important.

- A major change threatens four of Maslow's hierarchy of needs, i.e.
  - psychological, the need for food and shelter – person fears they may lose their job
  - safety, the need for a stable environment free from threat – even if their job remains secure, the person's environment is subject to change
  - love, the need to belong to groups
  - status, the need for self-respect and the esteem of peers – which can be threatened by a change because old skills are no longer valued and the person is worried that they will be unable to learn the new ones required.

- The only way to deal with the attack on a person's hierarchy of needs is to permit them to play some part in the decision-making process. People worry less if they believe that they have some influence over events.
- Herzberg's hygiene factors, such as the promise of increased salary or improved working conditions, will not motivate staff going through a change.
- To motivate staff, leaders should:
  - recognise and celebrate the staff's past achievements and express complete confidence in their ability to implement the change successfully and to be even better at their job in the future
  - give staff a degree of responsibility and freedom to act, within prescribed limits, for how they will implement the change.

Implications of learning for your leadership style

It has just struck me. Martin's latest tutorial was actually a microcosm of what leadership is all about. The job of a leader is to lead staff through change. Nothing ever remains static. Every school and college in the country is constantly involved in change and development. Change can be instigated by internal or external pressures. Wherever it comes from, the principal has to take responsibility for steering the organisation through the change. That's her job.

The tools she has for dealing with change are her ability to motivate staff and she can only do that if she can communicate with them. Therefore a leader's job comes down to identifying the destination (objectives) that she wants her followers to reach, and using all her skills to help them reach that destination. Once she has reached her goal she will barely have time to reflect on her followers' achievement before she has to start off on another journey.

So, sitting in an office doing 'my job' is not leading. At best, it's management and at worst, just plain old-fashioned administration. Now these functions are important and they have to be done. But if I'm to lead I have to free up more time in my diary for motivating and communicating with staff. How do I do that? Simple, I have to get out of the office and listen to what people have to say and respond to their worries and concerns. At the moment that's difficult because the principal has given me certain jobs that I have to do. Even so, I could find a bit of space in the diary for management by walking about (MBWA) if I put my mind to it.

Then when I become a principal my experience of MBWA will stand me in good stead and I can extend my leadership activities. But I'll have to guard against the all too human tendency to cling to the familiar. I will have to consciously delegate the type of administrative and managerial jobs that I'm currently doing and step out of my comfort zone and become the leader. Careful, I'm getting carried away. I can almost hear Wagner in the background!

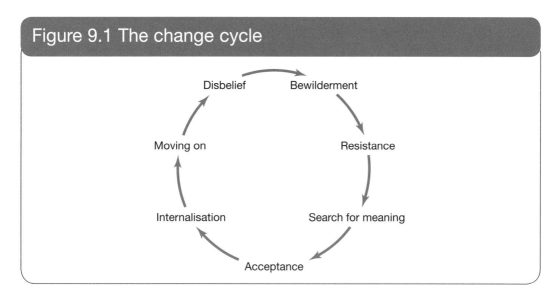

Figure 9.1 The change cycle

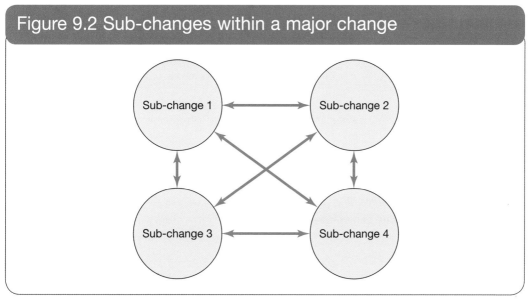

Figure 9.2 Sub-changes within a major change

Within any major change, such as the above, there will be a series of smaller changes. Each sub-change will reflect the same stages of change as outlined above.

Handout

Table 9.1 Stages in the change process

Stage	Stage descriptor	Explanation
1	Disbelief	Person is convinced that there has been a mistake and that nothing will change.
2	Bewilderment and anger	Person accepts that change is coming but can't understand why it is required or what their role will be in the future.
3	Resistance	Person digs their heels in and tries to stop or change what is proposed so as to have minimal effect on them and their role. They seek reasons to justify their belief that there is no reason why their role should change.
4	Searching	As the threat becomes firmed up the person identifies what their new role will be and consciously tries to amend it into a version of their old job.
5	Acceptance	Person comes to terms with the change and the new role that they will be asked to play but still hankers after the past.
6	Internalisation	The change has been implemented and the person has internalised both their changed duties and their redefined role in the school/college.
7	Moving on	The new role has become the norm and the person acts accordingly – until the next change.

Additional information on the issues covered by this tutorial can be found at/in:

● www.businessballs.com

● www.pearsoned.com/mcgrathandcoles

● **Fullen, M.** (1994) *Change Forces: Probing the depths of Education Reform.* London: The Falmer Press.

Ethics and leadership

Aim of tutorial

By the end of the tutorial you will be able to identify and start to develop your own ethical leadership style.

Contents

- Definition of ethics
- Who is the education leader's client?
- Ethical paradigms – teleological, deontological and character-based approaches
- The golden rule
- What constitutes ethical behaviour?
- Machiavelli and the ethics of power
- Machiavelli's top ten strategies for maintaining control and power
- Acting ethically

Nat's reflection

25 November

Sad to say, today is my last session with Martin. I've still not decided what I'll do next. A lot will depend on how my recent batch of applications for a principal's post are received. With any luck, I should have 2 or 3 interviews lined up after Christmas. Once they are out of the way and I know what I'm doing I'll make a decision. Maybe I can pick Martin's brain for ideas on how to blow the socks off an interview panel. Telling them that I'm a big fan of Showtime's friendly neighbourhood psychopath Dexter is probably not a good idea.

Martin agreed that we could look at leadership and ethics today. It's an area that I know virtually nothing about in a theoretical sense but which has caused me a few sleepless nights over the years. I've often had cause to ask myself: Did I act appropriately when I disciplined a member of staff? Or was it right for me to mislead management over a problem until I'd had time to sort it out? Or should I have delayed telling the staff about a reorganisation until everything had been put in place and staff were faced with a fait accompli? Maybe I'll get some answers today.

Review of tutorial

Martin had made me a cup of coffee, and what looked like the same dog-eared packet of biscuits that I had seen on my very first visit were on his desk when I entered. Next to his cup of tea was a copy of Machiavelli's *The Prince*. Martin saw me looking at the book and grinned. '**He get's a bad press**,' he said. '**The poor guy was just trying to make a living in the court of Lorenzo de Medici.**'

'If you say so,' I said and turned the recorder on.

'**OK. You wanted to talk about leadership and ethics today. So let's start with a definition of ethics. Ethics can be described as a set of moral principles or values that are intended to govern the conduct of a person. It's important to** realise that what is appropriate is determined by society and this can change over time. For example, in the 1950s homosexuality was a criminal offence; today it is an offence for a person or organisation to discriminate against a person based upon their sexual orientation. Therefore ethics is a social construct and can change over time.'

'Some religions would argue that they don't change and that it's society which changes.'

'That's because they deal in unchanging absolutes of a metaphysical nature.'

'OK,' I said.

'When someone talks about professional ethics, what they are referring to is the generally accepted professional standard of conduct or morality for that profession. Interestingly, the one feature that most professions explicitly state is that the practitioner must place the needs of his client before their own.'

'So if there is a conflict of interest, the practitioner should act in the best interests of their client and not their own interests.'

'Correct. Now why is that problematic in teaching?' Martin asked.

I sat and thought for a few moments and then remembered what Martin had said about the aims of education (Tutorial 1). 'In teaching, it is not entirely clear who the client is. Is it the learner, their parent, the government or the governors?'

'Precisely. Now in most educational cases it will be the learner, but what happens if the needs of the organisation come into conflict with the needs of the individual learner? For example, when the organisation has to save money and the only way to do that is reduce the number of teachers and increase the average class size. What would you do?'

'You're not going to like this, but throughout my career I've always done what I thought was in the best interests of the organisation.'

'Go on.'

'Well, I've always thought that management must act in the best interests of the organisation, because if they don't do that then the organisation could fail and possibly close. If that happens then all of the stakeholders in the organisation suffer.'

'So you are advocating a set of ethics based upon the greatest good for the greatest number of people. That's known as a utilitarian approach.'

'I suppose so. But I can see that not everyone would agree with me.'

'That's true, but at least you have tried to work out an ethical stance. You would be surprised how few people do that. It's really important for a leader to work out in advance what their ethical stance is. This is not easy to do because it requires you to examine what you believe in, what you stand for.'

'We're back to "know thyself", I said.

'Exactly. But let's try to build up a theory of ethics. Broadly speaking, there are two ethical paradigms. The first paradigm contains theoretical approaches that examine the person's conduct and the second considers the person's character.'

'OK. Can we start with conduct theories?' I asked.

'No problem. Your utilitarian approach is based upon consequences. In your world the greatest good for the greatest number makes your actions ethical. But you could also make an argument for ethical **egotism** which means that the leader should take decisions based upon what would be in her best interests. Or you could be **altruistic** and base your decisions on what would be the best interests of your followers, regardless of the effect on you as leader.'

'I can see how a utilitarian or altruistic approach can be ethical, but surely it can't be ethical for the leader to make decisions based upon maximising her outcomes.'

'Don't forget that ethics is a social construct. In some businesses it might be considered the norm for decisions to be made on the basis of the greatest good for the individual. For example, in a company that sought to maximise its profits and rewarded employees according to their contribution a leader would make decisions based upon personal interest, because what was good for them would be good for the company. Of course, this approach can go seriously wrong. There has been a lot of talk in financial circles that it was financial traders making decisions in their own best interests that caused the 2008 financial crisis.'

'OK, let me get this right,' I said, grabbing a piece of paper and scribbling down a simple chart. 'To summarise, there are three possible approaches and they are:

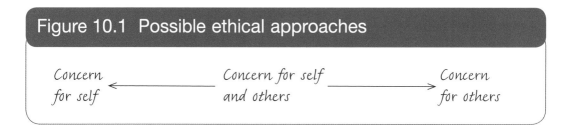

Figure 10.1 Possible ethical approaches

Concern for self ← Concern for self and others → Concern for others

'That's correct. Can you see what is common to all three approaches?

I examined what I had written, but I could see no connection between the three approaches. Shaking my head I said, 'Sorry.'

'That's OK, you're not a philosopher. What unites all three is that they are **teleological** based theories. This means that to determine whether the act is ethical or not the intended outcomes of the action are examined. In other words, if the intended outcomes were just and good, then the deed was ethical.'

'So teleological theories aren't concerned with how you achieved the results; they just look at the outcomes. That doesn't seem very ethical to me. It sounds like the old adage that the ends justify the means. In other words, it's all right to do evil as long as the results you achieve are virtuous.'

'So maybe you would prefer a **deontological** approach. Deontological approaches are concerned with duty and the actions of the leader. Simply put, every leader has a moral duty to act ethically. For example, leaders should tell the truth, avoid harming followers, respect the needs of followers and treat them fairly. These are all intrinsically good behaviours which leaders have a moral obligation to abide by.'

'But sometimes acting in such a way could do more harm than good. For example, always telling the truth. Jack Nicholson may have been morally bankrupt when he said in *A Few Good Men*, "You can't handle the truth" but he was also right. Many people can't handle knowing the full truth about themselves, their abilities or their standing in the organisation. In such cases, isn't it kinder to hide the full truth from them? I mean, as teachers, we do this all the time when giving feedback to learners: we emphasise the positives and sugar coat our criticisms.'

'That's why the deontological approach also says that a leader's actions would be ethical if the decisions she took did not breach their moral obligations, did not infringe the rights of her followers and if her actions supported or expanded the moral rights of others. Destroying someone by being too frank with them would not get past these requirements.'

'OK, so what about character-based approaches?'

'These are commonly known as virtue-based theories and revolve around the leader's character. Such theories focus on the actions of the leader, i.e. whether they display self-control, fairness, justice and honesty in their dealings with people and in their decision making.'

'They sound quasi religious in nature.'

'Indeed they are. All the great religious leaders such as Buddha, Christ and Mohammed stressed the need to reform ourselves and become virtuous before trying to impose our beliefs on others. Similarly Plato, Aristotle and the Stoics were interested in what constituted a virtuous life.'

'If they are character based, does that mean they link to trait theory?'

'No, I don't think so. One thing that writers in this area are in agreement on is that by practising these "virtues" they become part of the person's learned behaviour and are internalised to such an extent that they are manifested unconsciously in the person's everyday behaviour.'

'And traits can't be learnt.'

'Not according to trait theory. If I were to link it to any leadership theory it would have to be transformational leadership because, according to Burns, transformational leadership has a clear moral dimension, and it is this that separates it from all other leadership theories. Burns argued that leaders should help followers to identify, clarify and build their own moral values, with the values promoted by the leader impacting on the organisation and followers. '

Nat's reflection

26 November

I suppose that my approach has a teleological basis. I'm concerned with achieving the greatest good for the largest number of people. But if that's the case, why do I feel so badly when my approach delivers good results for twenty people but really bad results for one or two others? Am I being too sensitive? Do I need to come to terms with the fact that leadership requires me to decide between alternatives and that sometimes I have to choose the lesser of two evils.

Similarly, to what extent am I willing to accept that the ends justify the means? Can we ever justify using unethical means to achieve an ethical or good outcome? The Americans dropped atomic bombs on Hiroshima and Nagasaki, killing 100,000 people and injuring thousands more in order to end the war with Japan. It worked and it's ➡

estimated that it saved the lives of 250,000 American and Japanese soldiers and civilians who would have died had America been required to invade mainland Japan. But was it ethical?

If I'm going to sleep easy at night, I either need to:

- accept that I'm not willing to make decisions that fundamentally affect people's lives and stay in my present position

- identify clearly an ethical basis for taking decisions that I can live with.

This is going to require some serious thought.

Space for your notes

Prompts

- Have you ever worked for a manager or leader who you thought acted unethically? Which of their actions did you consider unethical? How did their actions make you feel?
- What ethical values do you bring to your professional life?

Review of tutorial

'Now that we've had a look at how ethical theories are organised, I'd like to spend some time examining those actions that people recognise almost instinctively as ethical. And those practices that people see as unethical but which occur regularly in every organisation.' I nodded in agreement and Martin continued, **'When dealing with individuals do you have any principles that govern how you treat them?'**

'I suppose I like to think that I follow the golden rule of "do unto others as you would have them do unto you". In other words treat people as you would like to be treated.'

'I suspect that most people subscribe to that teaching but very few manage to live up to it. What you are really talking about here is giving people unconditional respect. If you do that, you are never going to treat them as mere pawns in your search for advancement or achievement. Instead, you try to respect their decisions and listen to what they have to say. But what happens when you are faced with a conflict between the needs of the individual and those of the organisation? For example, you said you believe in preserving the organisation for the greater good of the largest number. That implies that you would be willing to sack someone if you thought it was in the best interests of the school. Am I right?'

'Yes,' I said with more conviction than I felt.

'OK, as long as you are clear about what your commitment to the organisation means in practice. What other ethical guidelines do you have for dealing with people?'

'I think leaders have a responsibility for the welfare of their followers. So, a bit like a doctor, I would first seek to do no harm to any learner or member of staff.'

'And how would you do that?'

'I'd try to avoid making decisions that were harmful to the staff and learners. And I'd ensure that the school's policies concerning equality, diversity, racism, respect for the individual, sexism and sexual orientation were understood and acted upon by all in the school.'

'And how would you achieve that?', Martin said.

'I'd seek to demonstrate my commitment to the policies by "walking the talk". In other words, demonstrate in my actions my commitment to the beliefs that underpin the policies.'

'Not a bad start. There are elements of respect and care for the followers in what you say as well as justice. By adhering to the organisation's policies on equality, you are seeking to treat followers and, I assume, learners in a fair and equal manner.'

'Absolutely. I certainly wouldn't want to be accused of treating staff unfairly. I've seen the problems that favouritism can cause. It really undermines the motivation of staff if they think that someone or some group is receiving special treatment.'

'You're quite correct when you say that leaders have to demonstrate a commitment to fairness. You can achieve this by enforcing the rules and regulations fairly and consistently. Staff need to see that no one is above the law. A valuable consequence of this is that staff will see that you are consistent in your actions and, as Goleman said, staff trust and follow leaders who are consistent.'

'All this enforcement of rules and regulations make me sound like a soulless bureaucrat.' I said.

'Maybe. But when you are walking the talk you should also enter into a genuine dialogue with the staff. Be as honest and open with staff as you can be. Listen to what they say – even when it's uncomfortable. That way, people will know that they can raise any subject with you and that will increase your standing and credibility with staff. Make sure that you don't hide behind misrepresentation or spin and never evade answering a question – leave that to politicians being interviewed on TV. However, there will always be some confidential or sensitive information that you can't share but the rest should be disseminated as widely as possible.'

'So what about the unethical behaviours?'

'I thought you'd never ask,' Martin said, rubbing his hands together in a pantomime imitation of Dickens' Fagan. 'Niccolo Machiavelli (1469–1527) was a diplomat whose most famous work *The Prince* was in effect a job application, written in the form of a letter and treatise to "The Magnificent Lorenzo De' Medici" of Florence. In it Machiavelli provides advice on how a ruling prince should conduct himself in affairs of state. His advice gave rise to the word "Machiavellian", which means cunning and deceitful behaviour and the philosophical view that the necessities of state transcend the demands of individual morality.'

'I don't know much about him but I think he argued that the ends justified the means,' I said.

'He did indeed. Basically he believed that might was right. Meaning that the Prince had the right to use all his powers to achieve his objectives, and that as he had been divinely appointed the Prince could not be judged on the basis of mere ethics. Over the centuries his views have been condemned by churchmen, politicians and business leaders as amoral and unethical. But many of his harshest critics have also been his most ardent students and used his advice to achieve and maintain power. But before you call them hypocrites, you need to remember that Machiavelli himself argues that, while it is important for a leader to demonstrate to the public that they are virtuous, it is not necessary for them to act in a virtuous manner. Proof that "spin" was not invented in the late twentieth century. Have you ever read *The Prince?*'

'No I'm afraid not.'

'Well I'd recommend it along with *The 48 Laws of Power*. Which, according to the *Sunday Times*, is the number one read of drug lords everywhere! I'm not for a moment suggesting that you should apply the dark arts that they propose, rather that you need to know about them if you are to guard yourself against those who do use the unethical practices to achieve their objectives.'

'You make it sound as if Voldemort is out to get me.'

'Oh, there are many people in the world who make Voldemort look like Willy Wonka. So here are my top tips from *The Prince*. First, leaders should always apply egotistical utilitarianism when deciding how to act or decide. All decisions should be based upon the maximisation of their welfare.'

'So much for my benign utilitarian approach.'

'Secondly, just as successful governments must be willing to act ruthlessly to achieve their ends, leaders must be willing to do whatever it takes to achieve their objectives, regardless of whom it harms. Thirdly, whether an action is unethical or not can only be judged in the light of what it was meant to achieve. If the aim is achieved the act is virtuous.'

'So therefore the leader is free to use any means available to achieve her objectives, provided she is successful, including dishonesty, lying, cheating and bullying?'

'That's about it.'

'Sounds like a principal I worked for before I became a teacher. She and the truth had never been introduced.'

'Fourthly, any new ruler who wishes to consolidate her power must destroy the family of the old prince.'

'We're back to the practice of newly appointed principals removing the threat posed by members of the previous principal's senior management team (Tutorial 2),' I said.

'Exactly. Members of the old SMT may resent the new principal and plot against her because they think that *they* should have been appointed principal. Or they may just impede her new ideas because they don't see any reason for changing the old procedures. Fifthly, whenever trouble is sensed, the Prince must act decisively and remove the threat before it has a chance to grow. In other words, any threat to the leader's position or authority must be killed at birth. A leader should always strike when the odds are in their favour. Any delay in taking decisive action can only benefit the opposition.'

'So crush all signs of dissent.'

'Well, you can either crush it or buy the conspirators off. The British Empire managed to maintain control of India for two centuries by bribing numerous maharajas and princes. A case of divide and rule. Similarly, a quick promotion can sideline a trouble maker and bind her to the leader. Sixthly, Machiavelli suggests that a wise prince will devise ways to ensure that his citizens are always dependent upon him and his authority. This suggests that the leader should create in her followers a feeling of dependency and gratitude for all that she has done for them. If staff think that they are incapable of surviving without the leader, they will lack the self-confidence required to challenge the leader's positions or views.'

''But you are going to end up with a flock of sheep,' I said.

'Very true but, from the leader's viewpoint, a flock of sheep is a lot less dangerous than a ravenous pack of wolves. The seventh principle is rather surprising. Machiavelli argues that a wise prince should never take things easy during times of peace but use the time to prepare for times of adversity. If you think about it, this approach ties in with Machiavelli's commitment to strategic thinking. It is only during slack periods that a leader has the time to eliminate any weaknesses in procedures or identify threats to her position and make plans to deal with them. Because once she is engaged in a battle, it is difficult to find the time to plan and think strategically. In such situations, there is the danger that the leader will react to events and, in doing so, make bad decisions that weaken her position.'

'Machiavelli clearly believed in forward planning.'

'Absolutely, but he warned against sticking too closely to a plan when circumstances had changed. He was the arch realist: he believed that princes had to deal with the reality that they found themselves in and not the reality they thought they would have to deal with or the one they wanted to deal with. Too many leaders fail to deal with the reality they face.'

'The principal I mentioned earlier was like that. The organisation was clearly in financial difficulties and the accountant reported to SMT that there would be a **cashflow** crisis in two months' time if action wasn't taken. He went as far as to say that the college was facing **insolvency**, meaning that it would be unable to pay its debts as they fell due. The principal latched on to this and demanded to know if the college was insolvent that day. Which of course it wasn't. She then basically ridiculed his claim that the college was or would ever be insolvent, because no one could predict the future.'

'Who was right?'

'Oh, the accountant was. Two months down the line, we couldn't pay the staff salaries and had to borrow money from the bank.'

'Who got the blame?'

'Do you really need to ask? The principal blamed it all on the poor old accountant.'

'That's what power can do to people. The eighth principle is that men are happy to break the bonds of love when it is to their advantage. However, they are less quick to break bonds based upon fear because they fear the possible punishments that follow. Again, what Machiavelli is saying is that it is impossible for a leader to be loved by every follower, and even those who express love and loyalty will desert if the price is right. As Judas did when he betrayed Jesus. Therefore it is better to be feared than loved because fear of retribution will bind followers to you more securely than love.'

'That's a fairly cynical view of human nature.'

'I'm not saying I agree with it. I'm just reporting what he said. Ninthly, while the prince should appear compassionate, faithful to his words, honest, frank and open, he should not deviate from what is in his best interests and should be willing to do evil if that is necessary. The important word in the statement is "appear". The leader should appear ethical but be willing to act unethically if that helps her achieve her objectives. Surprise is a valuable commodity in any struggle, and if the leader gives the impression of being ethical people will not expect her to act unethically. Of course, Machiavelli suggests that, if possible, the leader should arrange for the unethical act to be performed by a subordinate – who can then be sacked for acting so unethically.'

'I don't think I would have liked to work for Mr Machiavelli.'

'Well, surprisingly, he wasn't that successful as a diplomat. In football terms, Team Machiavelli was always sort of top of the Championship rather than a member of the Premier League.'

'A case of someone who couldn't rule – taught. Or, in this case, wrote,' I said mischievously.'

'If it wasn't for the fact that you are a teacher I might take exception to that comment,' Martin said with a smile. 'Anyway, his tenth principle at first sight appears to be contrary to common sense. Machiavelli suggests that princes, especially new ones, have often found that men who were suspect at the start of their rule, over time, become more loyal and more useful than those who, at the start, were trusted friends. Basically, he argues that friends can become resentful of your success, thinking that you owe them something for the support and help they have given you, whereas past enemies will be grateful for what you have given them and will seek to show their loyalty to you. Therefore the new leader should consider removing or sidelining "friends" when they come to power and replacing them with former "enemies".'

'That sort of contradicts the principles concerning dependency and fear of retribution. If followers are dependent on you or are terrified of what you might do, they are unlikely to challenge you.'

'There are some contradictions in what he says. But you have to remember that he is not suggesting that you apply all the principles all the same time, rather that you use them as separate strategies as and when they are required.'

'A sort of mix-and-match approach to unethical behaviour?'

'You've got it. Machiavelli's final principle was that, although a prince should consider the advice given to him, he should make it clear that he does not encourage or want people giving him advice when he has not asked for it. People offering advice are not in the best position to know what is in the best interests of the prince. Only he can know this. It is for the leader, not others, to determine when advice is required. The leader should be more willing to ask for advice on technical matters than strategic issues'.

Nat's reflection

27 November

In terms of what constitutes ethical actions, the 'Golden rule' is useful shorthand for describing how we should treat others. Everyone wants to be given a modicum of respect, told the truth, treated as valuable human beings and not just as a means to achieve the leader's objectives, asked for their opinions and allowed to provide input to major decisions that will affect them and their families. But, while we demand these considerations for ourselves, we don't always give them to the staff who work for us. I know I don't.

The odd thing is that I do genuinely try to treat staff as I want to be treated and yet I constantly fail. Usually, because I am under pressure and don't have the time to brief everyone and seek their input, or I'm just thoughtless and fail to realise that what I am doing may upset some staff. How much care and attention I can give to staff I'm not sure, but I know that I need to improve on the current level. Lack of time is really no excuse. The anger and trouble that a thoughtless act can engender often causes real problems. Valuable time then has to be spent trying to sort out the problem. Unfortunately, even when the matter is resolved, the member of staff often harbours feelings of resentment.

Hang on – I've just realised something. It's no good treating people as you want to be treated; you have to treat them as they want to be treated. Everyone will be different. Some people just want to do as they are told and don't want to be consulted on issues, others do. Others want to be treated like royalty and others are happy if you know their name and pass the time of day with them occasionally. The trick is working out an approach that will satisfy most of the people most of the time. I can never be 100 per cent successful, but I can think and act more strategically in order to demonstrate that I am trying to be ethical in how I deal with followers and take decisions.

Of course, if I adopted Machiavelli's approach, I could avoid all this soul-searching and just concentrate on what I want and what I want to achieve. But that is just not the type of person I am or want to be. I could use his ideas but my conscience would keep me awake at night. So a Machiavellian approach is not for me.

However, I need to recognise that many people are quite happy to use his ideas to get what they want. Just knowing some of the strategies that they can use should protect me. But if I do cross swords with such a person, how should I respond? Should I fight fire with fire or try to maintain my ethical standards? I'm not sure. But I suspect that knowing how angry I can get when I'm attacked I'm likely to respond in kind. But is that a good approach? If I'm not by nature a manipulative so-and-so, how well will I be able to use Machiavelli's strategies? It would probably be better if I gave some thought to how I can counter underhand tactics using strategies that I am comfortable with. Another case of 'To thy own self be true'.

Space for your notes

Prompts

- How do you expect to be treated at work?
- List five actions by management that make you feel that you are not respected as an individual.
- To what extent do you give unconditional respect to the people that work for you or that you work with?

Review of tutorial

'OK, we've had a general chat about what ethics is and where you stand. Now we need to consider what an education leader has to do to be considered an ethical leader. Any ideas?' Martin asked.

'Not be caught with her hand in the till,' I said only half jokingly.

'That's as good a place to start as any. Leaders have to be honest with themselves, their staff and the resources that they have at their disposal. Too many principals seem to think that the school or college resources are at their disposal.'

'I heard about one principal who built an extension to her house. She purchased all the materials required, but then used staff from the college's building department to construct the extension over the summer term. I don't know what deal she made with them but, whatever it was, it was on top of their normal salary.'

'I've heard similar tales and they have a corrosive impact on the organisation, because staff see what is going on and start to think that they too deserve a piece of the pie. Pretty soon everyone is running some scam for their own benefit. So it's vital that an ethical leader would challenge any unethical or dishonest behaviour as soon as they saw it.'

'What's that old Italian saying, a *fish stinks from the head?*'

'Old but still true. It is the principal that sets the ethical tone for any school or college. Mind you, it's no good being personally honest if you let dishonesty flourish around you. An ethical leader will adopt a zero tolerance to dishonesty. However, this should not just relate to the misuse of resources, it should also cover the relationship between managers and staff and supervisors and staff.'

'What do you mean?'

'The leader should demand that managers be honest in their dealings with all staff. If leaders are being frank and open with staff, then they have every right to demand that managers show the same level of candour with staff.'

'So you are trying to create an atmosphere in which people feel comfortable about speaking their mind?'

'Yes. There is evidence to indicate that staff are most influenced by their own line manager. So it's important that all managers display high ethical standards. It's this relationship that is the bedrock of the ethical organisation.'

'Anything else?' I asked.

'We've talked about being honest but leaders need to go further. It's no good being honest in what you tell people if you withhold important information. So transparency is vital. Leaders need to tell staff everything they need to know to understand the situation they find themselves in. Leaders should not put spin on the issues. Instead, they should report them accurately and then separately give their view of the situation. That way staff can make up their own mind.'

'So no **redacted** reports then!'

'Absolutely not. Leaders have to demonstrate trust and confidence in their followers. After all, trust is a two-way street. If one side shows a lack of trust it undermines the whole relationship.'

'Basically, what you are saying is that the leader should act as a role model when it comes to ethics.'

'Absolutely. Education leaders need to act as a role model for all staff, learners and other stakeholders. That's why it is essential that they take ultimate responsibility for any events that occur in their organisation. It's not good enough for them to say that they didn't know that bullying was rife in the school or that a teacher was acting inappropriately with one of the learners. Ultimately the buck stops with them.'

'It's not easy being the conscience of the organisation.'

'No it isn't. But someone has to do it and usually that someone is the principal. Now, you're not a principal yet, but you must have had one or two ethical dilemmas along the way. Care to share them?'

I did think of saying that it would be unethical for me to divulge them but thought better of it. 'I suppose that my main difficulties have involved balancing the needs of the organisation, staff, learners, governors and other stakeholders. Very often there is a conflict of interests.'

'So how do you deal with it? By deciding on what's best for the organisation?'

'There is always that option but very often the decision you have to make has no discernible effect on the organisation. It's just that one group gains at the expense of another.' I said.

'So how do you decide?'

'I like to think that after the organisation the learners come next, followed by the staff. But if I'm entirely honest, there have been occasions when I've ruled in favour of the staff rather than the learners.'

'In your scheme of ethics how did you justify that?'

'I suppose I used a form of cost–benefit analysis. I worked out what the benefits and cost of each course of action were on each group and then chose the course of action that minimised harm and maximised good across all groups.'

'It sounds very scientific,' Martin said.

'I wish it was. The truth is, it was a calculation I did in my head and was probably influenced by my own bias.'

'At least you are honest enough to admit it. The truth is that most decisions are made using the same informal calculus. There is very little certainty in the world of ethics. That's what makes ethics so difficult to deal with. Anyway, I think that's enough for today. Let me buy you a coffee and you can tell me what you plan to do in the future.'

Nat's reflection

29 November

It's not easy being an ethical leader. What's the old saying, 'Power corrupts and absolute power corrupts absolutely'. There are an awful lot of principals out there that think that their school or college is in fact their personal property and that they can run it any way they please. Over time, they start to believe that what is good for them has to be good for the school. I'm not sure how I can guard against the creeping corruption that accompanies such self-importance and arrogance.

Psychiatrists have ongoing therapy with other psychiatrists because of the dangers that their job poses. I could do with having a similar relationship with another principal – but I can't see that happening. No principal is ever going to admit weakness to another. No, I need to find a critical friend who would listen to what I have to say and challenge both my actions and the reasons for my decisions. Someone like Martin would be ideal or maybe a colleague who's now out of the game or retired. I'll have a think about it.

➡️

As for the list of ethical actions that Martin went through, I have to say that in the main I do abide by all of them. But I'm not always entirely consistent. Sometimes I am not as forthcoming and open with staff as I should be. I tend to keep things from them in the belief that I am protecting them from unnecessary worry. That sort of paternalistic attitude actually shows a lack of respect for the staff: I'm treating them as children rather than responsible adults.

Nor do I always challenge how other managers treat staff. In my defence, I suppose I could say that at the moment it's not my job to manage colleagues. But as principal it will be. I need to make it very clear to the members of my management team that I expect all managers to treat staff with respect and deal with them in an honest and open fashion.

Space for your notes

Prompts

- List the behaviours of managers and leaders in your organisation that make you feel that they do not respect you as an autonomous professional.
- List the behaviours of managers and leaders in your organisation that make you feel that they do respect you as an autonomous professional.

Record of tutorial

Summary notes from tutorial held on 25 November

- Ethics can be defined as a set of socially constructed moral principles or values intended to govern the conduct of individuals.

- Professional ethics normally demands that the practitioner place the welfare of their client above their own.

- It is essential that leaders identify a set of ethical standards that they are committed to as these should inform their actions.

- Ethical models can be classified as those based on either conduct or character.

- The conduct-based models can be described as either teleological in nature, that is concerned with outcomes, or deontological, which is concerned with the character of individuals.

- Teleological models include:
  - Utilitarianism – the leader's decisions are based upon producing the greatest good, in terms of results, for the greatest number of people.
  - Ethical egotism – the leader's decisions are based upon the greatest good, in terms of results, for his or her self.
  - Ethical altruism – the leader's decisions are based upon the greatest good, in terms of results, for others excluding the decision maker.

- Deontological models stress the need for the leader to do their duty and to act in such a way as to ensure that this is done. The leader's actions would be ethical if they did not breach their moral obligations.

- Character-based models suggest that actions are ethical if the leader demonstrates that they have acted virtuously by telling the truth, acting fairly, being honest and frank, showing no favouritism, being impartial and acting with integrity.

- By practising virtuous acts, proponents of character-based approaches argue that they become part of the person's learned behaviour and character and are ultimately revealed in the person's everyday actions.

- Actions that are considered intrinsically ethical are:
  - Following the golden rule – treating others as you wish to be treated.
  - Giving each individual unconditional respect.

- Acting in a just and fair fashion at all times.
- Showing no favouritism.
- Acting in a frank and open manner with people.
- Abiding by the rules laid down for all.
- Being scrupulously honest with the organisation's resources.
- Acting with integrity.

● Machiavelli argued that the needs of the state transcend the demands of individual morality, and that while it was necessary for the leader to demonstrate virtuous behaviour to the public it was not necessary to act virtuously.

● Machiavelli suggested that:
  - Leaders should act ruthlessly in defence of their interests.
  - If the act achieves its aim, it is virtuous: a case of the ends justifying the means.
  - New leaders should destroy the remnants of the old regime and thus avoid any possible conflict with supporters of the old order.
  - Whenever a leader suspects a challenge to their authority, they should destroy it immediately before it has a chance to grow.
  - Leaders should foster a culture of dependency among their followers, as this will reduce the chance of anyone challenging their position.
  - Leaders should use quiet periods to plan their strategy for dealing with possible future problem. Basically, a leader should not rest on their laurels.
  - Leaders must always deal with the reality that confronts them, not the one that they think exists or the one they wished existed.
  - Leaders should remember that the fear of retribution buys more loyalty than the bonds of love or friendship. It is therefore better to be feared than loved.
  - Leaders should remember that their previous friends and supporters can come to resent the leader's success and turn against them.
  - It is safer to trust an old enemy than an old friend, as the enemy will be grateful that the leader has appointed them to a position of trust and will be keen to demonstrate their loyalty at every opportunity.
  - Leaders should only listen to advice when they ask for it and not when others seek to prosper by offering it.

- An education leader should:
  - Set the ethical tone and standards for the entire institution and model what is acceptable behaviour.
  - Demonstrate absolute honesty in the use of the organisation's resources.
  - Communicate with staff in a frank and open manner.
  - Demonstrate trust and confidence in the staff.
  - Demand that line managers set an example to staff and act with integrity at all times.
  - Take ultimate responsibility for the actions of staff.
  - Apply the golden rule.

Implications of what I have learnt for my leadership style

I think there are four lessons that I can take from this session. First, there is no reason why I should not continue using a utilitarian approach to decision making. Most decisions made by leaders are about choosing between competing options and it is very rare that any one option will please all of the people. Therefore, it is a pragmatic and reasonable stance to try to take decisions that will produce the greatest good for the greatest number of people. Of course, there will be some occasions when a utilitarian approach is impractical or unjust and I will have to defend the needs of the minority, but such occasions are rare.

Secondly, I will follow Machiavelli's advice that leaders must deal with the reality facing them and not the reality that they wished existed. Too many leaders base their plans upon what they hope will be the situation and then fail to alter them when the reality is different. Of course, the problem is that I may be the last person to realise that I am living in a world of my own making. I must encourage staff to be open and frank with me and tell me the truth – even if I don't like it.

Thirdly, I will take responsibility for my decisions and actions. It seems to have become the norm in recent years for politicians and other leaders to blame everyone for mistakes except themselves. As President Truman said, 'The buck stops here'. If I abide by that rule, I think staff will respect me for it.

Fourthly, I will, as far as I can, apply the golden rule and try to treat people as I would like to be treated and as they expect to be treated. I'm sure to fail on occasions but at least I can try.

Figure 10.2 Ethical models of leadership

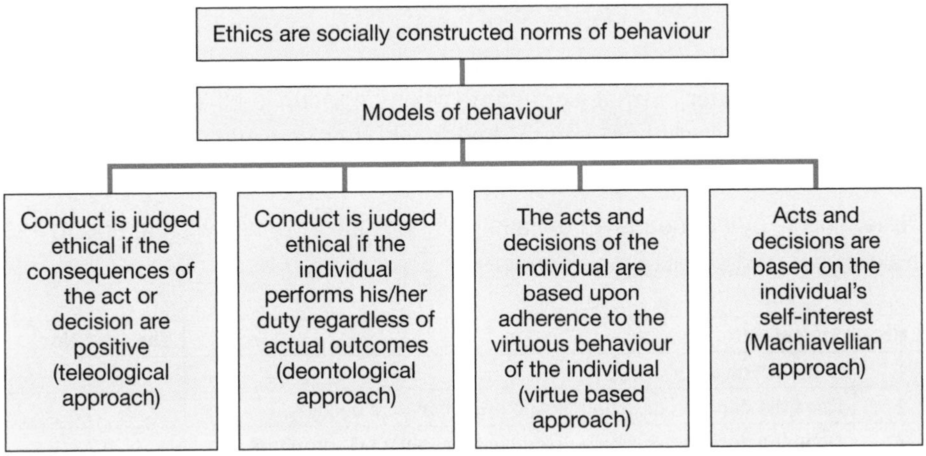

Ethics are socially constructed norms of behaviour

Models of behaviour

Conduct is judged ethical if the consequences of the act or decision are positive (teleological approach)	Conduct is judged ethical if the individual performs his/her duty regardless of actual outcomes (deontological approach)	The acts and decisions of the individual are based upon adherence to the virtuous behaviour of the individual (virtue based approach)	Acts and decisions are based on the individual's self-interest (Machiavellian approach)

Handout

Table 10.1 Ethical issues and decision making

In the busy world that education leaders inhabit, it is not always easy to find the time to consider to what extent a decision or action is ethical. The following 15-point checklist will help you to decide whether your actions are ethical or questionable.

Note: This is by no means an exhaustive checklist. You may wish to add to it to reflect your own situation and concerns.

No.	Statement	Yes	No
1	Is the action legal?		
2	Does the decision or action violate organisational policy?		
3	Does the decision or action discriminate against any group of people within the organisation?		
4	Have you put your interests above those of the organisation?		
5	Would you be happy for your decision or actions to be a matter of public record?		
6	Would you be happy for everybody to act as you have in this instance?		
7	Would you be happy if someone did this to you?		
8	Will the decision or course of action impact negatively upon your reputation?		
9	Is the decision or course of action consistent with your own espoused values and principles?		
10	Does your decision or course of action provide a good example to staff?		
11	Will the decision or course of action impact negatively upon the organisation's reputation?		
12	Will the decision or course of action impact negatively upon the values and behaviour of staff in the organisation?		
13	Will your decision or actions impact negatively upon the character of the organisation?		
14	Is the decision or course of action consistent with the organisation's espoused values and principles?		
15	Will the proposed course of action bring about a fair and just result?		

Your decision is likely to be ethical if you answered:

Yes to questions: 1, 5, 6, 7, 9, 10, 14, and 15

No to questions: 2, 3, 4, 8, 11, 12, and 13

Additional information on the issues covered by this tutorial can be found at/in:

- www.pearsoned.com/mcgrathandcoles
- **BERA** (2001) *Ethical Guidelines*. **www.bera.ac.uk/guidelines**
- **Machiavelli, N.** (1980) *The Prince*. Translated by Bull, G. Middlesex: Penguin Classics.
- **Vardy, P. and Grosch, P.** (1999) *The Puzzle of Ethics*. London: Harper Collins.

Glossary of terms

Ad hoc To improvise for a specific occasion.

Altruism (ethical) A devotion to and a concern for the welfare of others.

Andragogy The art and science of adult learning.

Assertiveness Positive and forceful presentation of one's self.

Balkanised cultures Just as there are numerous countries in the Balkans, each with its own unique culture and history, an organisation may contain several subcultures, each different from its neighbour.

Bloom's taxonomy A classification that identifies the three domains of learning, i.e. affective, cognitive and psychomotor, and the stages that a learner goes through from absolute beginner to expert within each domain.

Budget A financial plan prepared in advance that shows the organisation's income and expenditure for the financial year ahead. Also the amount of money that a budget holder is permitted to spend on a specified activity or resource.

Bureaucracy An organisation that is structured hierarchically and where decisions are based upon previously agreed procedures and protocols which have been written down.

Bureau-professional A system of management that existed in the public sector prior to 1980 which combined elements of bureaucracy and respect for the rights of professionals to operate in accordance with their professional practice.

Cashflow A record of the cash which is received and paid out by an organisation. Also a report that shows the existing and projected cash balances for the organisation.

CEO Chief executive officer of an organisation.

Change agents/champions A member of staff who may not be a supervisor or manager that recognises and supports the need for change and seeks to promote the change among colleagues.

Change management The supervision, by the responsible manager/s, of a significant change in how the organisation operates.

Charismatic leadership The ability of a person to exercise control over a group of people because they possess a complex mixture of personal qualities/traits.

Club culture A club or power culture is one in which the wishes of a single person or small group take precedence.

Collegiality/collegiate The situation, often in professional situations, where issues are discussed by all concerned as equals and decisions are based on agreement.

Constructive transactions The use of positive incentives in order to obtain compliance, e.g. praise, payment of a bonus or a promise of a promotion.

Contingency theory Contingency theory explores the relationship between the leader's personality, the level of structure inherent in the follower's job and the positional power of the leader.

Corrective transactions The use of negative incentives in order to obtain compliance, e.g. criticism, demotion or sacking.

Cost–benefit analysis A comparison of the benefits associated with completing a piece of work with the costs of undertaking the work. Very often the benefits are of a non-financial nature, such as pupil satisfaction, and it is necessary to find a way to give this a monetary value.

Cost centres A location unit to which costs can be charged, e.g. stationery or teaching salaries are charged to the Maths department.

Defender organisations Any organisation that seeks to minimise risk and adopts a cautious approach to management and decision making.

Deontological Deontological approaches to ethics suggest that conduct is ethical if the individual acts in accordance with his or her duties.

Discontinuous change Change which is not related to what has gone before. A sudden and unexpected change, e.g. the introduction of the internet which was unlike any communication system that had gone before.

Distributed leadership Distributed leadership exists within any group of individuals that are working together and recognises that knowledge and expertise are widely distributed in organisations, and that to maximise performance it is necessary to access these multiple sources.

Dyadic A group of two.

Emotional intelligence (EI) Emotional intelligence comprises five interlinked concepts: self-awareness, self-regulation, motivation, empathy and social skills.

Ethics The social, moral and professional conventions and beliefs that determine what is considered a righteous act.

Extrapolating To use past data to predict a future course of events.

Financial audit Annual audit of an organisation's trading, profit and loss account and balance sheet to determine if the accounts show a true and fair financial view of the organisation at a specific date.

Flat structures Organisations that have minimal levels of management between the front-line staff and senior management.

Great man theory The forerunner of trait theory which examined the lives of great men to identify what characteristics made them special.

Hawthorne experiments A series of experiments at the Hawthorne Plant in Chicago that explored the source of workers' motivation.

Hierarchical structures Organisations that have several levels of management between the front-line staff and senior management.

Hygiene factors Factors that demotivate staff if they are inadequate.

Ideology A self-contained system of beliefs, e.g. Marxism.

Insolvency A person or organisation that has insufficient money to pay their bills as they fall due.

Isomorphism A belief that the structures associated with commercial organisations are the most natural and effective way to coordinate the production of all goods and services.

Law of unintended consequences The belief that it is impossible to identify in advance all the effects that will occur as a result of a complex change.

Leader member exchange theory (LMX) A theory that examines the reciprocal relationship that exists between a leader and each individual subordinate.

Lean structures *See* flat structures.

Loose–tight control The practice whereby staff are given extensive freedom to act within a prescribed area.

Macro level High level, e.g. review of all secondary schools.

Micro level Low level, e.g. review of one school.

Management gurus Title given to writers on management who have come to be acknowledged by their readers as an insightful guide in the areas of management and leadership.

Managerialism An ideology that suggests that public sector organisations, including schools, hospitals and the police, should be run and managed using techniques and practices that are common in the private sector.

Organisational culture The basic assumptions, beliefs, expectations, norms and values that are shared by the members of the organisation and which operate at an unconscious level to define the organisation's view of itself.

Paradigm A philosophical or theoretical framework. A way of thinking and organising ideas into a coherent pattern.

Performance indicators Preset targets against which actual performance is compared and identified as acceptable or unacceptable.

Performativity A range of techniques used by management to influence the behaviour and outcomes achieved by either an individual or group at departmental or organisational level.

Person real or corporate The phrase used to identify those people and organisations that are viewed by the law as having a legal existence.

Professional autonomy The freedom given to a person to act in accordance with their professional training and ethics without constraint from outside forces.

Prospector organisations Organisations that are willing to embrace an element of risk in how they operate and take decisions.

Pseudo-transformational leaders Leaders who purport to be transformational but are not concerned with the needs of their followers and only interested in power and achievement of their own personal ambitions and desires, regardless of the cost to others.

Public choice theory (PCT) PCT argues that the market should be used as an instrument of regulation and control within the public sector.

Quasi-contracts Having the nature of a contract.

Redacted To edit or reduce prior to publication. For example, to remove or blank out passages of a work.

Schadenfreude Taking pleasure in the troubles of others.

Situational theory Theory which examines the interaction between situational variables and the leader's behaviour, with the leader supplying appropriate levels of support and/or direction depending on the needs of the follower.

SMT Senior management team.

Socialised The process of inculcating in an individual the values and norms of a group.

Stakeholders All those persons who have legitimate interest in the organisation.

Status quo The existing state of affairs.

Strategic compliers Those members of staff that accept that they must implement the requirements of senior management but make subtle changes to policy and processes in order to remain true to their own values and beliefs.

Strategic plan A plan that outlines the organisation's high-level aims and objectives in the mid to long term (typically 3 to 5 years).

Style theory Style theory is concerned with the leader's behaviour. The two main styles available to a leader are described as person (concern for staff) or task (concern for completion of the task) oriented.

Synergy The phenomenon that occurs when two or more resources are combined and produce results that exceed what would have been achieved if they remained independent. Often expressed as $2 + 2 = 5$.

Teleological Relating to ends or final outcomes; dealing with design or purpose, especially in natural phenomena.

360-degree appraisal The practice whereby a member of staff is appraised by his/her line manager, co-workers and subordinates.

Trading centres A subunit within an organisation to which both the income it generates and the costs it occurs are allocated. This enables the centre's profit or loss to be calculated.

Trait theory Theory which is concerned with the identification and analysis of the qualities of leaders.

Transactional leadership theory (TLX) Theory that suggests that leadership is a series of transactions between the leader and follower. Such transactions can be either corrective or constructive (see above).

Transformational leadership theory (TL) Transformational leadership is concerned with establishing a vision that attracts followers and helps them to go beyond the pursuit of their personal interests and, in so doing, raises their actions to a higher moral level.

Universalism Universalism holds that all organisations are basically the same and should pursue efficiency as the best means of satisfying their customers.

Unwilling compliers Unwilling compliance is characterised by the individual's rejection of the organisation's managerialist agenda.

Utilitarian A belief that decisions should be made on the basis of achieving the maximum good for the most possible people.

Value for money audit (VFM) The term VFM comprises economy, efficiency and effectiveness. Economy is concerned with obtaining resources at the least cost. Efficiency is concerned with maximising the outcome from a given input and effectiveness measures to what extent an organisation achieved its objectives.

Walk the talk Common jargon in business. Refers to the situation where the leader's actions match his/her words.

Willing compliers Willing compliance is characterised by the manager's wholehearted identification with institutional aims and objectives and the strategies used to achieve them. Such managers willingly embrace the managerialist agenda.

Bibliography

Asterisks indicate key texts.

Adair. J. (2002) *John Adair's 100 Greatest Ideas for Effective Leadership and Management.* Oxford: Capstone Publishing.

Avis, J. (1998) Discursive tricks, policy talk and the construction of teaching and learning within post-compulsory education in England. Paper presented to BERA Annual Conference. Belfast: Queen's University.

Ball, S.J. (1990) *Politics and Policy Making in Education: Explorations in Policy Sociology.* London: Routledge.

Ball, S.J. (2002) Performativities and fabrications in the education economy: Towards the performative society, in Gleeson, D. and Husbands, C. (eds) *The Performing School, Managing Teaching and Learning in a Performance Culture* (eds). London: Routledge/Falmer.

*****Ball, S.J.** (2003) The teacher's soul and the terrors of performativity, in *Journal of Education policy* 18(2): 215–28.

Bass, B.M. (1985) *Leadership and Performance Beyond Expectations.* New York: Free Press.

Bass, B.M. and Riggio R.E. (2006) *Transformational Leadership*, 2nd edn. New Jersey: Lawrence Erlbaum.

Bennett, N., Harvey, J.A., Wise, C. and Woods, P.A. (2002) *Distributed Leadership: A Desk Study Review (Draft).* Milton Keynes: The Open University.

*****Bennis, W. and Nanus, B.** (1985) *Leaders: The Strategies for Taking Charge.* New York: Harper and Row.

*****BERA** (2001) *Ethical Guidelines.* **www.bera.ac.uk/guidelines**.

Blake, R.R. and Mouton, J.S. (1985) *The Management Grid 3.* Houston,TX: Gulf Publishing.

*****Blanchard, K. with Carew, D. and Parisi-Carew, E.** (1996) *The One Minute Manager.* London: Harper Collins Business.

*****Blanchard, K., Zigarmi, P. and Zirgami, D.** (1985) *Leadership and the One Minute Manager.* London: Harper Collins.

Buchanan, J.M. (1986) *Liberty, Market and State: Political Economy in the 1980s.* Brighton: Wheatsheaf Books Ltd.

Burns, J.M. (1978) *Leadership*. New York: Harper & Row.

*Bush, T. (1995) *Theories of Educational Management,* 2nd edn. London: Paul Chapman Publishers.

*Cole, G.A. (2007) *Management Theory and Practice*, 6th edn. London: Thomson.

Covey, S. (2004) *The Seven Habits of Highly Effective People*, 15th edn. New York: Simon and Schuster.

Deal, T. and Kennedy, A. (1988) *Corporate Cultures: The Rites and Rituals of Corporate Life*. London: Penguin Books.

Deem, R. (1998) New managerialism and higher education: the management of performances and cultures in universities in the United Kingdom, *Studies in Sociology of Education* 8(1): 47–70.

Dunleavey, P. and Hood, C. (1994) From old public administration to new public management, *Public Money and Management*. July–September: 9–16.

Drucker, P. (1992) *The Age of Discontinuity*. New Jersey: Transaction Publishers.

Drucker, P. (2007) *The Practice of Management*. Oxford: Butterworth-Heinemann.

Drucker, P. (1999) *Management: Tasks, Responsibilities and Practices*. Oxford: Butterworth-Heinemann.

*Drucker, P. F. (1989) Why service institutions do not perform, in Riches, C. and Morgan, C. (eds) *Human Resource Management in Education*. Milton Keynes: Open University Press.

*Drucker, P. (2007) *The Essential Drucker*. Oxford: Butterworth-Heinemann.

Dunleavy, P. and Hood, C. (1994) From old public administration to new public management. In *Public Money and Management*, July–September: 9–16.

*Elliott, J. (2002) Characteristics of performative cultures: their central paradoxes and limitations as resources for educational reform', in Gleeson, D. and Husbands, C. (eds) *The Performing School: Managing Teaching and Learning in a Performance Culture*. London: Routledge/Falmer.

Fidler, B. (1997) School leadership: some key issues, in *School Leadership and Management* 17(1): 23–37.

Fidler, F. (1967) *A Theory of Leadership Effectiveness*. New York: McGraw Hill.

French, J. and Raven, B.H. (1960) The basis of social power, in Cartwright, D. (ed.) *Studies of Social Power*. Ann Arbor: Institute for Social Research.

Fullen, M. (1993) *Change Forces*. Bristol: The Falmer Press.

Fullen, M. (2009) *The Challenge of Change*. London: Corwin.

Giddens, A. (1997) *Sociology*, 3rd edn. Cambridge: Polity Press.

*Gleeson, D. and Shain, F. (1999) Managing ambiguity: between markets and managerialism – a case study of 'middle' managers in further education, *Sociological Review* 47(3): 461–90.

*Goleman, D. (1998) What makes a leader?, *Harvard Business Review*. Nov/Dec: 93–102.

*Goleman, D. (2000) Leadership that gets results, *Harvard Business Review*. March/April: 78–90.

Grace, E. (1995) *School Leadership*. London: Falmer Press.

Graen, G.B. and Uhl-Bien, M. (1991) The transformation of professionals into self-managing and partially self-designing contributions: towards a theory of leadership making, *Journal of Management Systems* 3(3): 33–44.

Gronn, P. (1996) From transactions to transformations. A New World order in the study of leadership in education, *Education Management and Administration* 24(1): 7–30.

*Gronn, P. (2002) Distributed leadership as a unit of analysis, *The Leadership Quarterly* 13: 423–51.

Gronn, P. (2003) Leadership: Who needs it? Lecture to the ESRC Seminar Series 'Challenging the orthodoxy of school leadership as a new theoretical perspective' at the School of Education, University of Birmingham. Birmingham: University of Birmingham.

Gunter, H.M. (2001) *Leaders and Leadership in Education*. London: Paul Chapman Publishers.

Handy, C. (1991) *Gods of Management*. London: Century Business.

Handy, C. (1992) The Language of leadership, in Syrett, M.S. and Hogg, C. (eds) *Frontiers of Leadership*. Oxford: Blackwell.

*Handy, C. (1993) *Understanding Organisations*, 4th edn. London: Penguin Books.

Handy, C. and Aitken, R. (1986) *Understanding Schools as Organisations*. London: Pelican.

Hargreaves, A. (1996) *Changing Teachers, Changing Times: Teachers' work and culture in the post modern age*. London: Cassell.

Hargreaves, D.H. (1995) School culture, school effectiveness and school improvement, *School Effectiveness and School Improvement* 6(1): 23–46.

*Harris, A. (2002) *Distributed leadership in schools: leading or misleading?* Paper presented at the British Educational Leadership and Management Association Annual Conference. Birmingham: University of Aston.

Hayek, F. ([1943] 1980) The facts of social science, in *Individualism and Economic Order*. Chicago: University of Chicago.

*Hayek, F. ([1944] 2007) *The Road to Serfdom: Text and Documents. The Definitive Edition*, Caldwell. B. (ed.) London: University of Chicago and Routledge.

Hayek, F.A. ([1952] 1991) *The Fatal Conceit: The Errors of Socialism*. Chicago: The University of Chicago Press.

Hayek, F. ([1960] 2006) *The Constitution of Liberty*. London: Routledge.

Hayek, F. ([1973] 1998) *Law, Legislation and Liberty*. London: Routledge.

Hayek, F.A. (1978) *New Studies in Philosophy, Politics, Economics and the History of Ideas*. London: Routledge & Kegan Paul.

Herzberg, F. (1993) *Motivation to Work*. New Jersey: Transaction Publishers.

Hodgkinson, C. (1991) *Education Management: The Moral Art*. New York: State University of New York Press.

Johnson, G. and Scholes, K. (1988) *Exploring Corporate Strategy*. London: Prentice Hall.

Knowles, M.S., Holton, E.F. and Swanson, R. (2005) *The Adult Learner: The Definitive Classic in Adult Education and Human Resource Development*. Oxford: Butterworth-Heinemann.

Kouzes, J. M. and Posner, B. Z. (2002) *The Leadership Challenge*, 3rd edn. San Francisco, CA: Jossey-Bass.

Law, S. and Glover, D. (2000) Educational Leadership and Learning. Buckingham: Open University Press.

Likert, R. (1961) *New Patterns of Management*. New York: McGraw-Hill.

*Lumby, J. (2002) *Distributed leadership in colleges: leading or misleading?* Paper presented at the British Educational Leadership and Management Association Annual Conference. Birmingham: Aston University.

*McBer, Hay (2000) *The Lessons of Leadership*. London: Hay Group Education.

*McGrath, J. (2004) Leading in a Managerialist Paradigm: A Survey of Perceptions within a Faculty of Education. Unpublished Ed D Thesis. Birmingham: Birmingham University.

McGregor, D. (1960) *The Human Side of Enterprise*, the Annotated Edition. London: McGraw Hill.

Maslow, A.H. (1998) *Maslow on Management*. New York: John Wiley and Son.

*Middlehurst, R. (1993) *Leading Academics*. Buckingham: Open University Press/SRHE.

Morgan, G. (1997) *Images of Organisation*, 2nd edn. London: Sage.

Moss-Kanter, R. (1988) *The Change Masters*. London: Unwin.

*Northouse, P. (2007) *Leadership Theory and Practice,* 4th edn. London: Sage.

Ogawa, R.T. and Bossert, S.T. (1995) Leadership as an organisational quality, *Educational Administration Quarterly* 31(2): 224–43.

*Olssen, M. and Peters, M.A. (2005) *Neo-liberalism, higher education and the knowledge economy: from the free market to knowledge capitalism*, in *The Journal of Education Policy* 20(3): 313–43.

Peters, T. and Austin, N. (1994) *A Passion for Excellence. The Leadership Difference.* London: Harper Collins.

Peters, T. and Waterman, R. (2004) *In Search of Excellence.* London: Profile Books.

Power, S. (1997) Managing the state and the market: new education management in Five Countries, *British Journal of Education* 45(4): 342–62.

Prichard, C. (1996) Making managers accountable or making managers?, *Educational Management and Administration* 24(1): 79–91.

*Randle, K. and Brady, N. (1997) Further education and new managerialism, *The Journal of Further and Higher Education.* 21(2): 229–39.

Reeves, J., Forde, C., O'Brien, J., Smith, P. and Tomlinson, H. (2002) *Performance Management in Education: Improving Practice.* London: Paul Chapman Publishing.

*Richmon, M.J. and Allison, D.J. (2003) Towards a conceptual framework for leadership enquiry, *Educational Management and Administration* 31(1): 31–50.

Rosenfield, R.H. and Wilson, D.C. (1999) *Managing Organisations: Texts, Readings and Cases*, 2nd edn. Berkshire: Mc Graw Hill.

Rutherford, D. (2002) *Sharing leadership and decision making.* Unpublished paper. Birmingham: University of Birmingham.

Schein, E. H. (1992) *Organisational Culture and Leadership*, 2nd edn. San Francisco: Jossey-Bass Publishers.

Simkins, T. (1999) Values, power and instrumentality: theory and research in education management, *Educational Management and Administration* 27(3): 267–81.

Simkins, T. (2000) Education reform and managerialism: comparing the experiences of schools and colleges, *Educational Management and Administration* 30(3): 293–12.

Southworth, G. (1998) *Leading Improving Primary Schools.* London: Falmer Press.

Stogdill, R.M. (1974) Handbook of Leadership: A Survey of Theory and Research. New York: Free Press.

Tichy, N.M. and DeVanna, M.A. (1986) *The Transformational Leader*, New York: John Wiley and Sons.

*Townsend, R. (1971) *Up the Organisation.* London: Coronet Books. Now out of print. Copies can be obtained from **www.abebooks.com** for a few pence.

Trowler, P. (1998) What managerialists forget: higher education credit framework and managerialist ideology, *International Studies in Sociology of Education* 8(1): 91–109.

TTA (1998) *National Standards for Headteachers.* London: Teachers Training Agency.

Vardy, P. and Grosch, P. (1999) *The Puzzle of Ethics.* London: Harper Collins.

Warren, B. (1998) On the curious notion of 'academic leadership': some philosophical considerations, *Higher Education Review* 30(2): 50–69.

Weber, M. (1924) Legitimate Authority and Bureaucracy in Organisation Theory: Selected Classic Readings, 5th edn (2007) D.S. Pugh (ed). London: Penguin Books.

*Winch, C. (2002) The economic aims of education, in *Journal of Philosophy of Education* 36(1): 101–117.

Winch. C. and Gingell, J. (2004) *Philosophy and Educational Policy: A Critical Introduction.* London: Routledge Falmer.

*www.businessballs.com

Index

The Classroom Gems series

Ready-made ideas, activities and games to transform any lesson or classroom in an instant.

www.pearson-books.com/classroomgems

9781408224359

9781408254172

9781408284841

9781405873925

9781405859455

9781408220382

9781408223208

9781408228098

9781408223260

9781408223291

9781408225608

9781408267745

9781408223239

9781408225516

9781408292051

9781408259344

9781408225578

9781408267776

Inspirational ideas for the Classroom

The Essential Guides series

Thorough, practical, and up-to-date advice on the core aspects of teaching and classroom strategies.

The Essential Guide to
Successful School Trips
John Trant
9781408204474

The Essential Guide to
Using ICT Creatively in the Primary Classroom
Steve Woods
9781408224977

The Essential Guide to
Classroom Assessment
Paul Dix
9781408230251

The Essential Guide to
Shaping Children's Behaviour in the Early Years
Lynn Cousins
9781408225028

The Essential Guide to
Secondary Teaching
Susan Davies
9781408224526

The Essential Guide to
Teaching 14–19 Diplomas
Lynn Senior
9781408225493

The Essential Guide to
Understanding Special Educational Needs
Jenny Thompson
9781408225004

The Essential Guide to
Taking Care of Behaviour (second edition)
Paul Dix
9781408225547

The Essential Guide to
Primary Teaching
Susan Davies
9781408225042

The Essential Guide to
Managing Teacher Stress
Bill Rogers
9781408261743

The Essential Guide to
Tackling Bullying
Michele Elliott
9781408264836

The Essential Guide to
Coaching and Mentoring (second edition)
Judith Tolhurst
9781408241721

The Essential Guide to
Lesson Planning (second edition)
Leila Walker
9781408253366

Practical Skills for Teachers
www.pearson-books.com/essentialguides